BIRDS OF THE ROCKIES

by

LEANDER S. KEYSER

Author of "In Bird Land," Etc.

With a Complete Check-List of Colorado Birds

Published September 27, 1902

TO KATHERINE AND THE BOYS

IN MEMORY OF MANY HAPPY DAYS BOTH INDOORS AND OUT

CONTENTS PAGE

BRIEF FOREWORD

With sincere pleasure the author would acknowledge the uniform courtesy of editors and publishers in permitting him to reprint many of the articles comprised in this volume, from the various periodicals in which they first appeared.

He also desires to express his special indebtedness to Mr. Charles E. Aiken, of Colorado Springs, Colorado, whose contributions to the ornithology of the West have been of great scientific value, and to whose large and varied collection of bird-skins the author had frequent access for the purpose of settling difficult points in bird identification. This obliging gentleman also spent many hours in conversation with the writer, answering his numerous questions with the intelligence of the scientifically trained observer. Lastly, he kindly corrected some errors into which the author had inadvertently fallen.

While the area covered by the writer's personal observations may be somewhat restricted, yet the scientific bird-list at the close of the volume widens the field so as to include the entire avi-fauna of Colorado so far as known to systematic students. Besides, constant comparison has been made between the birds of the West and the allied species and genera of our Central and Eastern States. For this reason the range of the volume really extends from the Atlantic seaboard to the parks, valleys, and plateaus beyond the Continental Divide.

L. S. K.

All are needed by each one; Nothing is fair or good alone. I thought the sparrow's note from heaven, Singing at dawn on the alder bough; I brought him home, in his nest, at even; He sings the song, but it cheers not now, For I did not bring home the river and sky;-- He sang to my ear,--they sang to my eye.

RALPH WALDO EMERSON: Each and All.

Not from his fellows only man may learn Rights to compare and duties to discern; All creatures and all objects, in degree, Are friends and patrons of humanity. There are to whom the garden, grove, and field Perpetual lessons of forbearance yield; Who would not lightly violate the grace The lowliest flower possesses in its place; Nor shorten the sweet life, too fugitive, Which nothing less than infinite Power could give.

WILLIAM WORDSWORTH: Humanity.

Sounds drop in visiting from everywhere-- The bluebird's and the robin's trill are there, Their sweet liquidity diluted some By dewy orchard spaces they have come.

JAMES WHITCOMB RILEY: A Child World.

Even in the city, I Am ever conscious of the sky; A portion of its frame no less Than in the open wilderness. The stars are in my heart by night, I sing beneath the opening light, As envious of the bird; I live Upon the payment, yet I give My soul to every growing tree That in the narrow ways I see. My heart is in the blade of grass Within the courtyard where I pass; And the small, half-discovered cloud Compels me till I cry aloud. I am the wind that beats the walls And wander trembling till it falls; The snow, the summer rain am I, In close communion with the sky.

PHILIP HENRY SAVAGE.

BIRDS OF THE ROCKIES

UP AND DOWN THE HEIGHTS

To study the birds from the level plains to the crests of the peaks swimming in cloudland; to note the species that are peculiar to the various altitudes, as well as those that range from the lower areas to the alpine heights; to observe the behavior of all the birds encountered in the West, and compare their habits, songs, and general deportment with those of correlated species and genera in the East; to learn as much as possible about the migratory movements up and down the mountains as the seasons wax and wane,--surely that would be an inspiring prospect to any student of the feathered fraternity. For many years one of the writer's most cherished desires has been to investigate the bird life of the Rocky Mountains. In the spring of 1899, and again in 1901, fortune smiled upon him in the most genial way, and--in a mental state akin to rapture, it must be confessed--he found himself rambling over the plains and mesas and through the deep canyons, and clambering up the dizzy heights, in search of winged rarities.

In this chapter attention will be called to a few general facts relative to bird life in the Rockies, leaving the details for subsequent recital. As might be expected, the towering elevations influence the movements of the feathered tenants of the district. There is here what might be called a vertical migration, aside from the usual pilgrimages north and south which are known to the more level portions of North America. The migratory journeys up and down the mountains occur with a regularity that amounts to a system; yet so far as regards these movements each species must be studied for itself, each having manners that are all its own.

In regions of a comparatively low altitude many birds, as is well known, hie to the far North to find the proper climatic conditions in which to rear their broods and spend their summer vacation, some of them going to the subarctic provinces and others beyond.

How different among the sublime heights of the Rockies! Here they are required to make a journey of only a few miles, say from five to one hundred or slightly more, according to the locality selected, up the defiles and canyons or over the ridges, to find the conditions as to temperature, food, nesting sites, etc., that are precisely to their taste. The wind blowing down to their haunts from the snowy summits carries on its wings the same keenness and invigoration that they would find if they went to British America, where the breezes would descend from the regions of snow and ice beyond the Arctic Circle.

It will add a little spice of detail if we take a concrete case. There is the handsome and lyrical white-crowned sparrow; in my native State, Ohio, this bird is only a migrant, passing for the summer far up into Canada to court his mate and rear his family. Now remember that Colorado is in the same latitude as Ohio; but the Buckeye State, famous as it is for furnishing presidents, has no lofty elevations, and therefore no white-crowns as summer residents. However, Colorado may claim this distinction, as well as that of producing gold and silver, and furnishing some of the sublimest scenery on the earth; for on the side of Pike's Peak, in a green, well-watered valley just below timber-line, I was almost thrown into transports at finding the white-crowns, listening to their rhythmic choruses, and discovering their grass-lined nests by the side of the babbling mountain brook. Altitude accomplishes for these birds what latitude does for their brothers and sisters of eastern North America.

There is almost endless variety in the avi-faunal life of the Rockies. Some species breed far above timber-line in the thickets that invade the open valleys, or clamber far up the steep mountain sides. Others ascend still higher, building their nests on the bald summits of the loftiest peaks at an altitude of fourteen thousand feet and more, living all summer long in an atmosphere that is as rare as it is refreshing and pure. Among these alpine dwellers may be mentioned the brown-capped leucostictes, which shall be accorded the attention they deserve in another chapter. Then, there are species which have representatives both on the plains and far up in the mountain parks and valleys, such as the western robin, the western meadow-lark, and the mountain bluebird.

In this wonderful country there is to be observed every style of migratory habit. A twofold migrating current must be noticed. While there is a movement up and down the mountain heights, there is at the same time a movement north and south, making the migratory system a perfect network of lines of travel. Some species summer in the mountains and winter on the plains; others summer in the mountains pass down to the plains in the autumn, then wing their way farther south into New Mexico, Mexico, Central America, and even South America, where they spend the winter, reversing this order on their return to the north in the spring; others simply pass through this region in their vernal and autumnal pilgrimages, stopping for a short time, but spending neither the summer nor the winter in this latitude; still others come down from the remote north on the approach of autumn, and winter in this State, either on the plains or in the sheltering ravines and forests of the mountains, and then return to the north in the spring; and, lastly, there are species that remain here all the year round, some of them in the mountains, others on the plains, and others again in both localities. A number of hardy birds--genuine feathered Norsemen--brave the arctic winters of the upper mountain regions, fairly revelling in the swirling snow-storms, and it must be a terrific gale indeed that will drive them down from their favorite habitats toward the plains.

Does the avi-fauna of the Rocky Mountain district differ widely from that of the Eastern States? The reply must be made in the affirmative. Therefore the first work of the bird-student from the

East will be that of a tyro--the identification of species. For this purpose he must have frequent recourse to the useful manuals of Coues and Ridgway, and to the invaluable brochure of Professor Wells W. Cooke on the "Birds of Colorado." In passing, it may be said that the last-named gentleman might almost be called the Colorado Audubon or Wilson.

In studying the birds of the West, one should note that there are western subspecies and varieties, which differ in some respects, though not materially, from their eastern cousins; for instance, the western robin, the western chipping sparrow, the western lark sparrow, and the western nighthawk. Besides, intermediate forms are to be met with and classified, the eastern types shading off in a very interesting process into the western. It would be impossible for any one but a systematist with the birds in hand to determine where the intermediate forms become either typical easterners or typical westerners.

Most interesting of all to the rambler on avian lore intent is the fact that there are many species and genera that are peculiar to the West, and therefore new to him, keeping him constantly on the qui vive. In Colorado you will look in vain for the common blue jay, so abundant in all parts of the East; but you will be more than compensated by the presence of seven other species of the jay household. The woodpeckers of the West (with one exception) are different from those of the East, and so are the flycatchers, the grosbeaks, the orioles, the tanagers, the humming-birds, and many of the sparrows. Instead of the purple and bronzed grackles (the latter are sometimes seen on the plains of Colorado, but are not common), the Rockies boast of Brewer's blackbird, whose habits are not as prosaic as his name would indicate. "Jim Crow" shuns the mountains for reasons satisfactory to himself; not so the magpie, the raven, and that mischief-maker, Clark's nutcracker. All of which keeps the bird-lover from the East in an ecstasy of surprises until he has become accustomed to his changed environment.

One cannot help falling into the speculative mood in view of the sharp contrasts between the birds of the East and those of the West. Why does the hardy and almost ubiquitous blue jay studiously avoid the western plains and mountains? Why do not the magpie and the long-crested jay come east? What is there that prevents the indigo-bird from taking up residence in Colorado, where his pretty western cousin, the lazuli finch, finds himself so much at home? Why is the yellow-shafted flicker of the East replaced in the West by the red-shafted flicker? These questions are more easily asked than answered. From the writer's present home in eastern Kansas it is only six hundred miles to the foot of the Rockies; yet the avifauna of eastern Kansas is much more like that of the Eastern and New England States than that of the Colorado region.

Perhaps the reason is largely, if not chiefly, physiological. Evidently there are birds that flourish best in a rare, dry atmosphere, while others naturally thrive in an atmosphere that is denser and more humid. The same is true of people. Many persons find the climate of Colorado especially adapted to their needs; indeed, to certain classes of invalids it is a veritable sanitarium. Others soon learn that it is detrimental to their health. Mayhap the same laws obtain in the bird realm.

The altitude of my home is eight hundred and eighty feet above sea-level; that of Denver, Colorado, six thousand one hundred and sixty, making a difference of over five thousand feet, which may account for the absence of many eastern avian forms in the more elevated districts. Some day the dissector of birds may find a real difference in the physiological structure of the eastern and western meadow-larks. If so, it is to be hoped he will at once publish his discoveries for the satisfaction of all lovers of birds.

If one had time and opportunity, some intensely interesting experiments might be tried. Suppose an eastern blue jay should be carried to the top of Pike's Peak, or Gray's, and then set free, how would he fare? Would the muscles and tendons of his wings have sufficient strength to bear him up in the rarefied atmosphere? One may easily imagine that he would go wabbling helplessly over the granite boulders, unable to lift himself more than a few feet in the air, while the pipit and the leucosticte, inured to the heights, would mount up to the sky and shout "Ha! ha!" in good-natured raillery at the blue tenderfoot. And would the feathered visitor feel a constriction in his chest and be compelled to gasp for breath, as the human tourists invariably do? It is even doubtful whether any eastern bird would be able to survive the changed meteorological conditions, Nature having designed him for a different environment.

INTRODUCTION TO SOME SPECIES

It was night when I found lodgings in the picturesque village of Manitou, nestling at the foot of the lower mountains that form the portico to Pike's Peak. Early the next morning I was out for a stroll along the bush-fringed mountain brook which had babbled me a serenade all night. To my delight, the place was rife with birds, the first to greet me being robins, catbirds, summer warblers, and warbling vireos, all of which, being well known in the East, need no description, but are mentioned here only to show the reader that some avian species are common to both the East and the West.

But let me pause to pay a little tribute to the brave robin redbreast. Of course, here he is called the "western robin." His distribution is an interesting scientific fact. I found him everywhere--on the arid plains and mesas, in the solemn pines of the deep gulches and passes, and among the scraggy trees bordering on timber-line, over ten thousand feet above sea-level. In Colorado the robins are designated as "western," forms by the system-makers, but, even though called by a modified title, they deport themselves, build their nests, and sing their "cheerily, cheerily, cheer up," just as do their brothers and sisters of the land toward the rising sun. If there is any difference, their songs are not so loud and ringing, and their breasts not quite so ruddy as are those of the eastern types. Perhaps the incessant sunshine of Colorado bleaches out the tints somewhat.

But in my ante-breakfast stroll at Manitou I soon stumbled upon feathered strangers. What was this little square-shouldered bird that kept uttering a shrill scream, which he seemed to mistake for a song? It was the western wood-pewee. Instead of piping the sweet, pensive "Pe-e-e-o-we-e-e-e" of the woodland bird of the Eastern States, this western swain persists in ringing the changes hour by hour upon that piercing scream, which sounds more like a cry of anguish than a song. At Buena Vista, where these birds are superabundant, their morning concerts were positively painful. One thing must be said, however, in defence of the western wood-pewee--he means well.

Another acquaintance of my morning saunter was the debonair Arkansas goldfinch, which has received its bunglesome name, not from the State of Arkansas, but from the Arkansas River, dashing down from the mountains and flowing eastwardly through the southern part of Colorado. Most nattily this little bird wears his black cap, his olive-green frock, and his bright yellow vest. You will see at once that he dresses differently from the American goldfinch, so well known in the East, and, for that matter, just as well known on the plains of Colorado, where both species dwell in harmony. There are some white markings on the wings of Spinus psaltria that give them a gauze-like appearance when they are rapidly fluttered.

His song and some of his calls bear a close resemblance to those of the common goldfinch, but he is by no means a mere duplicate of that bird; he has an individuality of his own. While his flight is undulatory, the waviness is not so deeply and distinctly marked; nor does he sing a cheery cradle-song while swinging through the ether, although he often utters a series of unmusical chirps. One of the most pleasingly pensive sounds heard in my western rambles was the little coaxing call of this bird, whistled mostly by the female, I think. No doubt it is the tender love talk of a young wife or mother, which may account for its surpassing sweetness.

Every lover of feathered kind is interested in what may be called comparative ornithology, and therefore I wish to speak of another western form and its eastern prototype--Bullock's oriole, which in Colorado takes the place of the Baltimore oriole known east of the plains all the way to the Atlantic coast. However, Bullock's is not merely a variety or subspecies, but a well-defined species of the oriole family, his scientific title being Icterus bullocki.

Like our familiar Lord Baltimore, he bravely bears black and orange; but in bullocki the latter color invades the sides of the neck, head, and forehead, leaving only a small black bow for the throat and a narrow black stripe running back over the crown and down the back of the neck; whereas in Icterus galbula the entire head and neck are black. Brilliant as Bullock's oriole is, he does not seem to be anxious to display his fineries, for he usually makes it a point to keep himself ensconced behind a clump of foliage, so that, while you may hear a desultory piping in the trees, apparently inviting your confidence, it will be a long time before you can get more than a provoking glimpse of the jolly piper himself. "My gorgeous apparel was not made for parade," seems to be his modest disclaimer.

He is quite a vocalist. Here is a quotation from my lead-pencil, dashes and all: "Bullock's oriole--fine singer--voice stronger than orchard oriole's--song not quite so well articulated or so elaborate, but louder and more resonant--better singer than the Baltimore." It might be added that Bullock's, like the orchard, but unlike the Baltimore, pipes a real tune, with something of a theme running through its intermittent outbursts. The plumage of the young bird undergoes some curious changes, and what I took to be the year-old males seemed to be the most spirited musicians.

Maurice Thompson's tribute to the Baltimore oriole will apply to that bird's western kinsman. He calls him:--

"Athlete of the air-- Of fire and song a glowing core;"

and then adds, with tropical fervor:

"A hot flambeau on either wing Rimples as you pass me by; 'T is seeing flame to hear you sing, 'T is hearing song to see you fly.

* * * * *

"When flowery hints foresay the berry, On spray of haw and tuft of brier, Then, wandering incendiary, You set the maple swamps afire!"

Many nests of Bullock's oriole rewarded my slight search. They are larger and less compactly woven than the Baltimore's, and have a woolly appearance exteriorly, as if the down of the Cottonwood trees had been wrought into the fabric. Out on the plains I counted four dangling nests, old and new, on one small limb; but that, of course, was unusual, there being only one small clump of trees within a radius of many miles.

In the vicinity of Manitou many trips were taken by the zealous pedestrian. Some of the dry, steep sides of the first range of mountains were hard climbing, but it was necessary to make the effort in order to discover their avian resources. One of the first birds met with on these unpromising acclivities was the spurred towhee of the Rockies. In his attire he closely resembles the towhee, or "chewink," of the East, but has as an extra ornament a beautiful sprinkling of white on his back and wings, which makes him look as if he had thrown a gauzy mantle of silver over his shoulders.

But his song is different from our eastern towhee's. My notes say that it is "a cross between the song of the chewink and that of dickcissel," and I shall stand by that assertion until I find good reason to disown it--should that time ever come. The opening syllabication is like dickcissel's; then follows a trill of no specially definable character. There are times when he sings with more than his wonted force, and it is then that his tune bears the strongest likeness to the eastern towhee's. But his alarm-call! It is no "chewink" at all, but almost as close a reproduction of a cat's mew as is the catbird's well-known call. Such crosses and anomalies does this country produce!

On the arid mountain sides among the stunted bushes, cactus plants, sand, and rocks, this quaint bird makes his home, coming down into the valleys to drink at the tinkling brooks and trill his roundelays. Many, many times, as I was following a deep fissure in the mountains, his ditty came dripping down to me from some spot far up the steep mountain side--a little cascade of song mingling with the cascades of the brooks. The nests are usually placed under a bush on the sides of the mesas and mountains.

And would you believe it? Colorado furnishes another towhee, though why he should have been put into the Pipilo group by the ornithologists is more than I can tell at this moment. He has no analogue in the East. True, he is a bird of the bushes, running sometimes like a little deer from one clump to another; but if you should see him mount a boulder or a bush, and hear him sing his rich, theme-like, finely modulated song, you would aver that he is closer kin to the thrushes or thrashers than to the towhees. There is not the remotest suggestion of the towhee minstrelsy in his prolonged and well-articulated melody. It would be difficult to find a finer lyrist among the mountains.

But, hold! I have neglected to introduce this pretty Mozart of the West. He is known by an offensive and inapt title--the green-tailed towhee. Much more appropriately might he be called the chestnut-crowned towhee, for his cope is rich chestnut, and the crest is often held erect, making him look quite cavalier-like. It is the most conspicuous part of his toilet. His upper parts are grayish-green, becoming slightly deeper green on the tail, from which fact he derives his common name. His white throat and chin are a further diagnostic mark. The bright yellow of the edge of the wings, under coverts and axillaries is seldom seen, on account of the extreme wariness of the bird.

In most of the dry and bushy places I found him at my elbow--or, rather, some distance away, but in evidence by his mellifluous song. Let me enumerate the localities in which I found my little favorite: Forty miles out on the plain among some bushes of a shallow dip; among the foothills about Colorado Springs and Manitou; on many of the open bushy slopes along the cog-road leading to Pike's Peak, but never in the dark ravines or thick timber; among the bushes just below timber-line on the southern acclivity of the peak; everywhere around the village of Buena Vista; about four miles below Leadville; and, lastly, beyond the range at Red Cliff and Glenwood.[1]

[1] This list was greatly enlarged in my second trip to Colorado in 1901.

The song, besides its melodious quality, is full of expression. In this respect it excels the liquid chansons of the mountain hermit thrush, which is justly celebrated as a minstrel, but which does not rehearse a well-defined theme. The towhee's song is sprightly and cheerful, wild and free, has the swing of all outdoors, and is not pitched to a minor key. It gives you the impression that a bird which sings so blithesome a strain must surely be happy in his domestic relations.

Among the Rockies the black-headed grosbeak is much in evidence, and so is his cheerful, good-tempered song, which is an exact counterpart of the song of the rose-breasted grosbeak, his eastern kinsman. Neither the rose-breast nor the cardinal is to be found in Colorado, but they are replaced by the black-headed and blue grosbeaks, the former dwelling among the lower mountains, the latter occurring along the streams of the plains. Master black-head and his mate are partial to the scrub oaks for nesting sites. I found one nest with four callow bantlings in it, but, much to my grief and anger, at my next call it had been robbed of its precious treasures. A few days later, not far from the same place, a female was building a nest, and I am disposed to believe that she was the mother whose children had been kidnapped.

Instead of the scarlet and summer tanagers, the Rocky Mountain region is honored with that beautiful feathered gentleman, the Louisiana tanager, most of whose plumage is rich, glossy yellow, relieved by black on the wings, back, and tail; while his most conspicuous decoration is the scarlet or crimson tinting of his head and throat, shading off into the yellow of the breast. These colors form a picturesque combination, especially if set against a background of green. The crimson staining gives him the appearance of having washed his face in some bright-red pigment, and like an awkward child, blotched his bosom with it in the absence of a napkin.

So far as I could analyze it, there is no appreciable difference between his lyrical performances and those of the scarlet tanager, both being a kind of lazy, drawling song, that is slightly better than no bird music at all. One nest was found without difficulty. It was placed on one of the lower branches of a pine tree by the roadside at the entrance to Engleman's Canyon. As a rule, the males are not excessively shy, as so many of the Rocky Mountain birds are. The tanagers were seen far up in the mountains, as well as among the foothills, and also at Red Cliff and Glenwood on the western side of the Divide.

A unique character in feathers, one that is peculiar to the West, is the magpie, who would attract notice wherever he should deign to live, being a sort of grand sachem of the outdoor aviary. In some respects the magpies are striking birds. In flight they present a peculiar appearance; in fact, they closely resemble boys' kites with their long, slender tails trailing in the breeze. I could not avoid the impression that their tails were superfluous appendages, but no doubt they serve the birds a useful purpose as rudders and balancing-poles. The magpie presents a handsome picture as he swings through the air, the iridescent black gleaming in the sun, beautifully set off with snowy-white trimmings on both the upper and lower surfaces of the wings. On the perch or on the wing he is an ornament to any landscape. As to his voice--well, he is a genuine squawker. There is not, so far as I have observed, a musical cord in his larynx and I am sure he does not profess to be a musical genius, so that my criticism will do him no injury. All the use he has for his voice seems to be to call his fellows to a new-found banquet, or give warning of the approach of an interloper upon his chosen preserves. His cry, if you climb up to his nest, is quite pitiful, proving that he has real love for his offspring. Perhaps the magpies have won their chief distinction as architects. Their nests are really remarkable structures, sometimes as large as fair-sized tubs, the framework composed of good-sized sticks, skilfully plaited together, and the cup lined with grass and other soft material, making a cosey nursery for the infantile magpies. Then the nest proper is roofed over, and has an entrance to the apartment on either side. When you examine the structure closely, you find that it fairly bristles with dry twigs and sticks, and it is surprising how large some of the branches are that are braided into the domicile. All but one of the many nests I found were deserted, for my visit was made in June, and the birds, as a rule, breed earlier than that month. Some were placed in bushes, some in willow and cottonwood trees, and others in pines; and the birds themselves were almost ubiquitous, being found on the plains, among the foothills, and up in the mountains as far as the timber-line, not only close to human neighborhoods, but also in the most inaccessible solitudes.

[2] In this volume the author has made use of the terminology usually employed in describing bird music. Hence such words as "song," "chant," "vocal cords," etc., are of frequent occurrence. In reality the writer's personal view is that the birds are whistlers, pipers, fluters, and not vocalists, none of the sounds they produce being real voice tones. The reader who may desire to go into this matter somewhat technically is referred to Maurice Thompson's chapter entitled "The Anatomy of Bird-Song" in his "Sylvan Secrets," and the author's article, "Are Birds Singers or Whistlers?" in "Our Animal Friends" for June, 1901.

In one of my excursions along a stream below Colorado Springs, one nest was found that was still occupied by the brooding bird. It was a bulky affair, perhaps half as large as a bushel basket, placed in the crotch of a tree about thirty feet from the ground. Within this commodious structure was a globular apartment which constituted the nest proper. Thus it was roofed over, and had an entrance at each side, so that the bird could go into his house at one doorway and out at the other, the room being too small to permit of his turning around in it. Thinking the nest might be occupied, in a tentative way I tossed a small club up among the branches, when to my surprise a magpie sprang out of the nest, and, making no outcry, swung around among the trees, appearing quite nervous and shy. When she saw me climbing the tree, she set up such a heart-broken series of cries that I permitted sentiment to get the better of me, and clambered down as fast as I could, rather than prolong her distress. Since then I have greatly regretted my failure to climb up to the nest and examine its contents, which might have been done without the least injury to the owner's valuable treasures. A nestful of magpie's eggs or bairns would have been a gratifying sight to my bird-hungry eyes.

One bird which is familiar in the East as well as the West deserves attention on account of its choice of haunts. I refer to the turtle dove, which is much hardier than its mild and innocent looks would seem to indicate. It may be remarked, in passing, that very few birds are found in the deep canyons and gorges leading up to the higher localities; but the doves seem to constitute the one exception to the rule; for I saw them in some of the gloomiest defiles through which the train scurried in crossing the mountains. For instance, in the canyon of the Arkansas River many of them were seen from the car window, a pair just beyond the Royal Gorge darting across the turbulent stream to the other side. A number were also noticed in the darkest portions of the canyon of the Grand River, where one would think not a living creature could coax subsistence from the bare rocks and beetling cliffs. Turtle doves are so plentiful in the West that their distribution over every available feeding ground seems to be a matter of social and economic necessity.

BALD PEAKS AND GREEN VALES

One of my chief objects in visiting the Rockies was to ascend Pike's Peak from Manitou, and make observations on the birds from the base to the summit. A walk one afternoon up to the Halfway House and back--the Halfway House is only about one-third of the way to the top--convinced me that to climb the entire distance on foot would be a useless expenditure of time and effort. An idea struck me: Why not ride up on the cog-wheel train, and then walk down, going around by some of the valleys and taking all the time needed for observations on the avi-faunal tenantry? That was the plan pursued, and an excellent one it proved.

When the puffing cog-wheel train landed me on the summit, I was fresh and vigorous, and therefore in excellent condition physically and mentally to enjoy the scenery and also to ride my hobby at will over the realm of cloudland. The summit is a bald area of several acres, strewn with immense fragments of granite, with not a spear of grass visible. One of the signal-station men asked a friend who had just come up from the plain, "Is there anything green down below? I'd give almost anything to see a green patch of some kind." There was a yearning strain in his tones that really struck me as pathetic. Here were visitors revelling in the magnificence of the panorama, their pulses tingling and their feelings in many cases too exalted for expression; but those whose business or duty it was to remain on the summit day after day soon found life growing monotonous, and longed to set their eyes on some patch of verdure. To the visitors, however, who were in hale physical condition, the panorama of snow-clad ranges and isolated peaks was almost overwhelming. In the gorges and sheltered depressions of the old mountain's sides large fields of snow still gleamed in the sun and imparted to the air a frosty crispness.

When the crowd of tourists, after posing for their photographs, had departed on the descending car, I walked out over the summit to see what birds, if any, had selected an altitude of fourteen thousand one hundred and forty-seven feet above sea-level for their summer home. Below me, to the east, stretched the gray plains running off to the skyline, while the foothills and lower mountains, which had previously appeared so high and rugged and difficult of access, now seemed like ant-hills crouching at the foot of the giant on whose crown I stood. Off to the southwest, the west, and the northwest, the snowy ranges towered, iridescent in the sunlight. In contemplating this vast, overawing scene, I almost forgot my natural history, and wanted to feast my eyes for hours on its ever-changing beauty; but presently I was brought back to a consciousness of my special vocation by a sharp chirp. Was it a bird, or only one of those playful little chipmunks that abound in the Rockies? Directly there sounded out on the serene air another ringing chirp, this time overhead, and, to my delight and surprise, a little bird swung over the summit, then out over the edge of the cliff, and plunged down into the fearsome abyss of the "Bottomless Pit." Other birds of the same species soon followed his example, making it evident that this was not a birdless region. Unable to identify the winged aeronauts, I clambered about over the rocks of the summit for a while, then slowly made my way down the southern declivity of the mountain for a short distance. Again my ear was greeted with that loud, ringing chirp, and now the bird uttering it obligingly alighted on a stone not too far away to be seen distinctly through my binocular. Who was the little waif that had chosen this sky-invading summit for its summer habitat? At first I mistook it for a horned lark, and felt so sure my decision was correct that I did not look at the bird as searchingly as I should have done, thereby learning a valuable lesson in thoroughness. The error was corrected by my friend, Mr. Charles E. Aiken, of Colorado Springs, who has been of not a little service in determining and classifying the avian fauna of Colorado. My new-found friend (the feathered one, I mean) was the American pipit, which some years ago was known as the tit-lark.

"Te-cheer! te-cheer! te-cheer!" (accent strong on the second syllable) the birds exclaimed in half-petulant remonstrance at my intrusion as I hobbled about over the rocks. Presently one of them darted up into the air; up, up, up, he swung in a series of oblique leaps and circles, this way and that, until he became a mere speck in the sky, and then disappeared from sight in the cerulean depths beyond. All the while I could hear his emphatic and rapidly repeated call, "Te-cheer! te-cheer!" sifting down out of the blue canopy. How long he remained aloft in "his watch-tower in the skies" I do not know, for one cannot well count minutes in such exciting circumstances, but it seemed a long time. By and by the call appeared to be coming nearer, and the little aeronaut swept down with a swiftness that made my blood tingle, and alighted on a rock as lightly as a snowflake. Afterwards a number of other pipits performed the same aerial exploit. It was wonderful to see them rise several hundred feet into the rarefied atmosphere over an abyss so deep that it has been named the "Bottomless Pit."

The pipits frequently flitted from rock to rock, teetering their slender bodies like sandpipers, and chirping their disapproval of my presence. They furnished some evidence of having begun the work of nest construction, although no nests were found, as it was doubtless still too early in the season. In some respects the pipits are extremely interesting, for, while many of them breed in remote northern latitudes, others select the loftiest summits of the Rockies for summer homes, where they rear their broods and scour the alpine heights in search of food. The following interesting facts relative to them in this alpine country are gleaned from Professor Cooke's pamphlet on "The Birds of Colorado":

In migration they are common throughout the State, but breed only on the loftiest mountains. They arrive on the plains from the South about the last of April, tarry for nearly a month, then hie to the upper mountain parks, stopping there to spend the month of May. By the first of June they have ascended above timber-line to their summer home amid the treeless slopes and acclivities. Laying begins early in July, as soon as the first grass is started. Most of the nests are to be found at an elevation of twelve thousand to thirteen thousand feet, the lowest known being one on Mount Audubon, discovered on the third of July with fresh eggs. During the breeding season these birds never descend below timber-line. The young birds having left the nest, in August both old and young gather in flocks and range over the bald mountain peaks in quest of such dainties as are to the pipit taste. Some of them remain above timber-line until October although most of them have by that time gone down into the upper parks of the mountains. During this month they descend to the plains, and in November return to their winter residence in the South.

While watching the pipits, I had another surprise. On a small, grassy area amid the rocks, about a hundred feet below the summit, a white-crowned sparrow was hopping about on the ground, now leaping upon a large stone, now creeping into an open space under the rocks, all the while picking up some kind of seed or nut or insect. It was very confiding, coming close to me, but vouchsafing neither song nor chirp. Farther on I shall have more to say about these tuneful birds, but at this point it is interesting to observe that they breed abundantly among the mountains at a height of from eight thousand to eleven thousand feet, while the highest nest known to explorers was twelve thousand five hundred feet above the sea. One of Colorado's bird men has noted the curious fact that they change their location between the first and second broods-- that is, in a certain park at an elevation of eight thousand feet they breed abundantly in June, and then most of them leave that region and become numerous among the stunted bushes above timber-line, where they raise a second brood. It only remains to be proved that the birds in both localities are the same individuals, which is probable.

On a shoulder of the mountain below me, a flock of ravens alighted on the ground, walked about awhile, uttered their hoarse croaks, and then took their departure, apparently in sullen mood. I could not tell whether they croaked "Nevermore!" or not.

Down the mountain side I clambered, occasionally picking a beautiful blossom from the many brilliant-hued clusters and inhaling its fragrance. Indeed, sometimes the breeze was laden with the aroma of these flowers, and in places the slope looked like a cultivated garden. The only birds seen that afternoon above timber-line were those already mentioned. What do the birds find to eat in these treeless and shrubless altitudes? There are many flies, some grasshoppers, bumble-bees, beetles, and other insects, even in these arctic regions, dwelling among the rocks and in the short grass below them watered by the melting snows.

At about half-past four in the afternoon I reached the timber-line, indicated by a few small, scattering pines and many thick clumps of bushes. Suddenly a loud, melodious song brought me to a standstill. It came from the bushes at the side of the trail. Although I turned aside and sought diligently, I could not find the shy lyrist. Another song of the same kind soon reached me from a distance. Farther down the path a white-crowned sparrow appeared, courting his mate. With crown-feathers and head and tail erect, he would glide to the top of a stone, then down into the grass where his lady-love sat; up and down, up and down he scuttled again and again. My approach put an end to the picturesque little comedy. The lady scurried away into hiding, while the little prince with the snow-white diadem mounted to the top of a bush and whistled the very strain that had surprised me so a little while before, farther up the slope. Yes, I had stumbled into the summer home of the white-crowned sparrow, which on the Atlantic coast and the central portions of the American continent breeds far in the North.

It was not long before I was regaled with a white-crown vesper concert. From every part of the lonely valley the voices sounded. And what did they say? "Oh, de-e-e-ar, de-e-ar, Whittier, Whittier," sometimes adding, in low, caressing tones, "Dear Whittier"--one of the most melodious tributes to the Quaker poet I have ever heard. Here I also saw my first mountain bluebird, whose back and breast are wholly blue, there being no rufous at all in his plumage. He was feeding a youngster somewhere among the snags. A red-shafted flicker flew across the vale and called, "Zwick-ah! zwick-ah!" and then pealed out his loud call just like the eastern yellow-shafted high-holder. Why the Rocky Mountain region changes the lining of the flicker's wings from gold to crimson--who can tell? A robin--the western variety--sang his "Cheerily," a short distance up the hollow, right at the boundary of the timber-line.

About half-past five I found myself a few hundred feet below timber-line in the lone valley, which was already beginning to look shadowy and a little uncanny, the tall ridges that leaped up at the right obscuring the light of the declining sun. My purpose had been to find accommodations at a mountaineer's cabin far down the valley, in the neighborhood of the Seven Lakes; but I had tarried too long on the mountain, absorbed in watching the birds, and the danger now was that, if I ventured farther down the hollow, I should lose my way and be compelled to spend the night alone in this deserted place. I am neither very brave nor very cowardly; but, in any case, such a prospect was not pleasing to contemplate. Besides, I was by no means sure of being able to secure lodgings at the mountaineer's shanty, even if I should be able to find it in the dark. There seemed to be only one thing to do--to climb back to the signal station on the summit.

I turned about and began the ascent. How much steeper the acclivities were than they had seemed to be when I came down! My limbs ached before I had gone many rods, and my breath came short. Upward I toiled, and by the time my trail reached the cog-road I was ready to drop from exhaustion. Yet I had not gone more than a third of the way to the top. I had had no supper, but was too weary even to crave food, my only desire being to find some place wherein to rest. Night had now come, but fortunately the moon shone brightly from a sky that was almost clear, and I had no difficulty in following the road.

Wearily I began to climb up the steep cog-wheel track. Having trudged around one curve, I came to a portion of the road that stretched straight up before me for what seemed an almost interminable distance, and, oh! the way looked so steep, almost as if it would tumble back upon my head. Could I ever drag myself up to the next bend in the track? By a prodigious effort I did this at last--it seemed "at last" to me, at all events--and, lo! there gleamed before me another long stretch of four steel rails.

My breath came shorter and shorter, until I was compelled to open my mouth widely and gasp the cold, rarefied air, which, it seemed, would not fill my chest with the needed oxygen. Sharp pains shot through my lungs, especially in the extremities far down in the chest; my head and eye-balls ached, and it seemed sometimes as if they would burst; my limbs trembled with weakness, and I tottered and reeled like a drunken man from side to side of the road, having to watch carefully lest I might topple over the edge and meet with a serious accident. Still that relentless track, with its quartette of steel rails, stretched steep before me in the distance.

For the last half mile or more I was compelled to fling myself down upon the track every few rods to rest and recover breath. Up, up, the road climbed, until at length I reached the point where it ceases to swing around the shoulders of the mountain, and ascends directly to the summit. Here was the steepest climb of all. By throwing my weary frame on the track at frequent intervals and resting for five minutes, taking deep draughts of air between my parched lips, I at last came in sight of the government building. It is neither a mansion nor a palace, not even a cottage, but never before was I so glad to get a glimpse of a building erected by human hands. It was past nine o'clock when I staggered up to the door and rang the night bell, having spent more than three hours and a half in climbing about two miles and a half. Too weary to sleep, I tossed for hours on my bed. At last, however, "nature's sweet restorer" came to my relief, and I slept the deep sleep of unconsciousness until seven o'clock the next morning, allowing the sun to rise upon the Peak without getting up to greet him. That omission may have been an unpardonable sin, for one of the chief fads of visitors is to see the sun rise from the Peak; but I must say in my defence that, in the first place, I failed to wake up in time to witness the Day King's advent, and, in a second place, being on bird lore intent rather than scenic wonders, my principal need was to recruit my strength for the tramping to be done during the day. The sequel proved that, for my special purpose, I had chosen the wiser course.

By eight o'clock I had written a letter home, eaten a refreshing breakfast, paying a dollar for it, and another for lodging, and was starting down the mountain, surprised at the exhilaration I felt, in view of my extreme exhaustion of the evening before. I naturally expected to feel stiff and sore in every joint, languid and woe-be-gone; but such was not the case. It is wonderful how soon one recovers strength among these heights. How bracing is the cool mountain air, if you breathe it deeply! As I began the descent, I whistled and sang,--that is, I tried to. To be frank, it was all noise and no music, but I must have some way of giving expression to the uplifted emotions that filled my breast. Again and again I said to myself, "I'm so glad! I'm so glad! I'm so glad!" It was gladness pure and simple,--the dictionary has no other word to express it. No pen can do justice to the panorama of mountain and valley and plain as viewed from such a height on a clear, crisp morning of June. One felt like exclaiming with George Herbert:

"Sweet day, so cool, so calm, so bright, The bridal of the earth and sky!"

So far as the aesthetic value of it went, I was monarch of all I surveyed, even though mile on mile of grandeur and glory was spread out before me. The quatrain of Lowell recurred to my mind:

"'Tis heaven alone that is given away, 'Tis only God may be had for the asking; No price is set on the lavish summer; June may be had by poorest comer."

Before leaving the Peak, I watched a flock of birds eating from the waste-heap at the Summit House. They were the brown-capped rosy finches, called scientifically Leucosticte australis. Their plumage was a rich chocolate, suffused over neck, breast, and back with intense crimson, while the pileum was quite black. With one exception--the white-tailed ptarmigan--they range the highest in summer of all Colorado birds. They are never seen below timber-line in that season, and are not known to breed below twelve thousand feet; thence to the tops of the highest peaks they hatch and rear their young. In August old and young swarm over the summits picking edible insects from the snow, while in winter they descend to timber-line, where most of them remain to brave the arctic weather and its frequent storms.

Bidding a regretful good-by to the summit, for it held me as by a magician's spell, I hastened down the steep incline of the cog-wheel road, past Windy Point, and turning to the right, descended across the green slope below the boulder region to the open, sunlit valley which I had visited on the previous afternoon. It was an idyllic place, a veritable paradise for birds. Such a chorus as greeted me from the throats of I know not how many white-crowned sparrows,--several dozen, perhaps,--it would have done the heart of any lover of avian minstrelsy good to listen to. The whole valley seemed to be transfigured by their roundelays, which have about them such an air of poetry and old-world romance. During the morning I was so fortunate as to find a nest, the first of this species that I had ever discovered. Providence had never before cast my lot with these birds in their breeding haunts. The nest was a pretty structure placed on the ground, beneath a bush amid the green grass, its holdings consisting of four dainty, pale-blue eggs, speckled with brown. The female leaped from her seat as I passed near, and in that act divulged her little family secret. Although she chirped uneasily as I bent over her treasures, she had all her solicitude for nothing; the last thing I would think of doing would be to mar her maternal prospects. As has been said, in this valley these handsome sparrows were quite plentiful; but when, toward evening, I clambered over a ridge, and descended into the valley of Moraine Lake, several hundred feet lower than the Seven Lakes valley, what was my surprise to find not a white-crown there! The next day I trudged up to the Seven Lakes, and found the white-crowns quite abundant in the copses, as they had been farther up the hollow on the previous day; and, besides, in a boggy place about two miles below Moraine Lake there were several pairs, and I was fortunate enough to find a nest. Strange--was it not?--that these birds should avoid the copsy swamps near Moraine Lake, and yet select for breeding homes the valleys both above and below it. Perhaps the valley of Moraine Lake is a little too secluded and shut in by the towering mountains on three sides, the other places being more open and sunshiny.

The upper valley was the summer home of that musician par excellence of the Rockies, the green-tailed towhee, and he sang most divinely, pouring out his

"full heart In profuse strains of unpremeditated art."

Having elsewhere described his minstrelsy and habits with more or less fulness, I need give him only this passing reference here. A little bird with which I here first made acquaintance was an elegant species known as Audubon's warbler, which may be regarded as the western representative of the myrtle warbler of the East. The two birds are almost counterparts. Indeed, at first I mistook the Audubon for the myrtle. The former has a yellow throat, while the latter's throat is white.

In all the upper mountain valleys, and on the steep slopes of the western as well as the eastern side of the Divide, I had the Audubon warblers often at my elbow. In summer they make their homes at an altitude of seven to eleven thousand feet, and are partial to pine timber; indeed, I think I never found them elsewhere, save occasionally among the quaking asps. I learned to distinguish Audubon's chanson from those of his fellow-minstrels. It is not much of a song--a rather weak little trill, with a kind of drawl in the vocalization that forms its diagnostic feature. The persistency with which it is repeated on the solitary pine-clad mountain sides constitutes its principal charm.

The winter haunts of Audubon's warblers are farther south than Colorado, mostly in Mexico and Guatemala, although a few of them remain in the sheltered mountain valleys of the western part of the United States. Early in May they appear on the plains of eastern Colorado, where they are known only as migrants. Here a double movement presently takes place--what might be called a longitudinal and a vertical migration--one division of the warbler army sweeping north to their breeding grounds in Canada, and the other wheeling westward and ascending to the alpine heights among the mountains, where they find the subartic conditions that are congenial to their natures without travelling so great a distance. Here they build their nests in the pine or spruce trees, rear their families, and as autumn approaches, descend to the plains, tarry there a week or two, then hie to their winter homes in the South.

One of the most gorgeous tenants of this valley was Wilson's warbler.[3] It wears a dainty little cap that is jet black, bordered in front and below with golden yellow, while the upper parts are rich olive and the lower parts bright yellow. These warblers were quite abundant, and were evidently partial to the thickets covering the boggy portions of the vale. While Audubon's warblers kept themselves for the most part among the pines on the slopes and acclivities, the little black-caps preferred the lower ground. Their songs were not brilliant performances, though rather pleasing, being short, jerky trills, somewhat lower in the scale than those of the well-known summer warbler.

[3] Mr. Aiken says, "The Rocky Mountain representative of Wilson's warbler is an intermediate form, nearest the Pacific coast bird which is distinguished as the pileolated warbler."

While I was stalking about in the low, boggy part of the hollow, my attention was attracted by an odd little song that came rolling down from the pines on the mountain side. At length, time was found to go to the place whence the song came. What could the gay little minstrel be? Somewhere I had heard such minstrelsy--but where? There were runs in it that bore some resemblance to certain strains of the Carolina wren's vigorous lays, but this songster's voice was of a finer quality and had less volume than that of the Carolina. The little bird was found flitting among the pines, and continued to sing his gay little ballad with as much vigor as before. Indeed, my presence seemed to inspire him to redouble his efforts and to sing with more snap and challenge. He acted somewhat like a wren, but was smaller than any species of that family with which I was acquainted, and no part of his plumage was barred with brown and white.

Now the midget in feathers leaped up the alternating branches of a pine, and now he flew down and fluttered amid the chaos of dead logs and boughs on the ground, all the while rolling his ditty from his limber tongue. Beginning with an exceedingly fine whistle, which could not be heard far away, he descanted in sounds that it is impossible to convey in syllables. The best literation of his song that I was able to make was the following: "Tse-e-ek, tse-e-ek, tse-e-e-ek, cholly-cholly-cholly, che-che-che, pur-tie, pur-tie, pur-tie!" the pur-tie accented strongly on the second syllable and the whole performance closing with an interrogative inflection.

For a long time I watched the little acrobat, but could not settle his identity. Some hours later, while stalking along the other side of the valley, I heard the song duplicated; this time the singer elevated his crest feathers, and at once I recognized him; he was the ruby-crowned kinglet, of course, of course! It was a shame not to identify him at first sight. In Ohio I had often heard his song during the migrating season, and now remembered it well; but never dreaming that the ruby-crown would be found in these alpine districts, I was completely thrown off my reckoning on hearing his quaint melodies.

The ruby-crowned kinglet migrates to these heights in the spring and rears his brood at an elevation of from nine thousand feet to the timber-line, building a nest far up in a pine tree; whereas his eastern kindred hie to the northern part of the United States and beyond, to find summer homes and suitable breeding grounds. Within their chosen boundaries the rubies are very plentiful in the Rockies, their quaint rondeaus tumbling down from every pine-clad acclivity. In October they descend to the plains, and in the latter part of the month hurry off to a more southerly clime.

The birds were most abundant in the upper part of the valley, keeping close to the precipitous heights of the Peak. It was a long walk down to the mountaineer's cabin, and I had reason to be glad for not having undertaken to find it the evening before, as I should certainly have lost my way in the darkness. No one was at home now, but through the screen door I could see a canary in a cage. Not a very inviting place to spend the night, I reflected, and I crossed the valley, climbed a steep ridge, following a slightly used wagon road, and trudged down the other side into what I afterwards found was the valley of Moraine Lake, one of the crystal sheets of water that are seen from the summit of Pike's Peak sparkling in the sunshine. While climbing the ridge, I saw my first mountain chickadee, capering about in the trees. He called like the familiar black-cap, and his behavior was much like that bird's. As will be seen in another chapter, I afterwards heard the mountain chickadee's song on the western side of the range, and found it to be quite unlike the minor strain of our pleasant black-cap of the East.

On the mountain side forming the descent to Moraine Lake a flock of Clark's nutcrackers were flying about in the pine woods, giving expression to their feelings in a great variety of calls, some of them quite strident. A little junco came in sight by the side of the trail, and hopped about on the ground, and I was surprised to note a reddish patch ornamenting the centre of his back. Afterwards I learned that it was the gray-headed junco, which is distinctly a western species, breeding among the mountains of

Colorado. Thrashing about among some dead boles, and making a great to-do, were a pair of small woodpeckers, which closely resembled the well-known downies of our eastern longitudes. I suppose them to have been their western representatives, which are known, according to Mr. Aiken and Professor Cooke, as Batchelder's woodpecker. Near the same place I saw a second pair of mountain bluebirds, flitting about somewhat nervously, and uttering a gentle sigh at intervals; but as evening was now rapidly approaching, I felt the need of finding lodging for the night, and could not stop to hunt for their nest.

Faring down the mountain side to the lake, I circled around its lower end until I came to the cottage of the family who have the care of the reservoirs that supply the three towns at the foot of the mountains with water fresh from the snow-fields. Here, to my intense relief, I was able to secure lodging and board as long as I desired to remain.

I enjoyed the generous hospitality offered me for two nights and considerably more than one day. It was a genuine retreat, right at the foot of a tall mountain, embowered in a grove of quaking asps. Several persons from Colorado Springs, one of them a professor of the college, were spending their outing at the cottage, and a delightful fellowship we had, discussing birds, literature, and mountain climbing.

After resting awhile, I strolled up the valley to listen to the vesper concert of the birds, and a rich one it was. The western robins were piping their blithesome "Cheerilies," Audubon's warblers were trilling in the pines, and, most of all--but here I had one of the most gratifying finds in all my mountain quest. It will perhaps be remembered that the white-crowned sparrows, so plentiful in the upper valley, were not to be seen in the valley of Moraine Lake. Still there were compensations in this cloistered dip among the towering mountains; the mountain hermit thrushes--sometimes called Audubon's thrushes--found the sequestered valley precisely to their liking, and on the evening in question I saw them and heard their pensive cadences for the first time. Such exquisite tones, which seemed to take vocal possession of the vale and the steep, pine-clad mountain side, it has seldom been my good fortune to hear. Scores of the birds were singing simultaneously, some of their voices pitched high in the scale and others quite low, as though they were furnishing both the air and the contralto of the chorus. It was my first opportunity to listen to the songs of any of the several varieties of hermit thrushes, and I freely confess that I came, a willing captive, under the spell of their minstrelsy, so sweet and sad and far away, and yet so rich in vocal expression. In the latter part of the run, which is all too brief, there is a strain which bears close resemblance to the liquid melody of the eastern wood-thrush, but the opening notes have a pathetic quality all their own. Perhaps Charles G. D. Roberts can give some idea of one's feelings at a time like this:

"O hermit of evening! thine hour Is the sacrament of desire, When love hath a heavenlier flower, And passion a holier fire."

A happy moment it was when a nest of this mountain hermit was discovered, saddled on one of the lower limbs of a pine and containing four eggs of a rich green color. These birds are partial to dense pine forests on the steep, rocky mountain sides. They are extremely shy and elusive, evidently believing that hermit thrushes ought to be heard and not seen. A score or more may be singing at a stone's throw up an acclivity, but if you clamber toward them they will simply remove further up the mountain, making your effort to see and hear them at close range unavailing. That evening, however, as the gloaming settled upon the valley, one selected a perch on a dead branch some distance up the hillside, and obligingly permitted me to obtain a fair view of him with my glass.

The hermits breed far up in the mountains, the greatest altitude at which I found them being on the sides of Bald Mountain, above Seven Lakes and a little below the timber-line. To this day their sad refrains are ringing in my ears, bringing back the thought of many half-mournful facts and incidents that haunt the memory.

A good night's rest in the cottage, close beneath the unceiled roof, prepared the bird-lover for an all-day ramble. The matutinal concert was early in full swing, the hermit thrushes, western robins, and Audubon's warblers being the chief choralists. One gaudy Audubon's warbler visited the quaking asp grove surrounding the cottage, and trilled the choicest selections of his repertory. Farther up the valley several Wilson's warblers were seen and heard. A shy little bird flitting about in the tangle of grass and bushes in the swampy ground above the lake was a conundrum to me for a long time, but I now know that it was Lincoln's sparrow, which was later found in other ravines among the mountains. It is an exceedingly wary bird, keeping itself hidden amid the bushy clusters for the greater part of the time, now and then venturing to peep out at the intruder, and then bolting quickly into a safe covert. Occasionally it will hop out upon the top of a bush in plain sight, and remain for a few moments, just long enough for you to fix its identity and note the character of its pleasing trill. Some of these points were settled afterwards and not on the morning of my first meeting with the chary little songster.

My plan for the day was to retrace my steps of the previous afternoon, by climbing over the ridge into the upper valley and visiting the famous Seven Lakes, which I had missed the day before through a miscalculation in my direction. Clark's crows and the mountain jays were abundant on the acclivities. One of the latter dashed out of a pine bush with a clatter that almost raised the echoes, but, look as I would, I could find no nest or young or anything else that would account for the racket.

The Seven Lakes are beautiful little sheets of transparent water, embosomed among the mountains in a somewhat open valley where there is plenty of sunshine. They are visible from the summit of Pike's Peak, from which distant viewpoint they sparkle like sapphire gems in a setting of green. As seen from the Peak they appear to be quite close together, and the land about them seems perfectly level, but when you visit the place itself, you learn that some of them are separated from the others by ridges of considerable height. Beautiful and sequestered as the spot is, I did not find as many birds as I expected. Not a duck or water bird of any kind was seen. Perhaps there is too much hunting about the lakes, and, besides, winged visitors here would have absolutely no protection, for the banks are free of bushes of any description, and no rushes or flags grow in the shallower parts. On the ridges and mountain sides the kinglets and hermit thrushes were abundant, a robin was caroling, a Batchelder woodpecker chirped and pounded in his tumultuous way, Clark's crows and several magpies lilted about, while below the lakes in the copses the white-crowned sparrows and green-tailed towhees held lyrical carnival, their sway disputed only by the natty Wilson's warblers.

It was a pleasure to be alive and well in such a place, where one breathed invigoration at every draught of the fresh, untainted mountain air; nor was it less a delight to sit on the bank of one of the transparent lakes and eat my luncheon and quaff from a pellucid spring that gushed as cold as ice and as sweet as nectar from the sand, while the white-crowned sparrows trilled a serenade in the copses.

Toward evening I clambered down to the cottage by Moraine Lake. The next morning, in addition to the birds already observed in the valley, I listened to the theme-like recitative of a warbling vireo, and also watched a sandpiper teetering about the edge of the water, while a red-shafted flicker dashed across the lake to a pine tree on the opposite side. As I left this attractive valley, the hermit thrushes seemed to waft me a sad farewell.

A little over half a day was spent in walking down from Moraine Lake to the Halfway House. It was a saunter that shall never be forgotten, for I gathered a half day's tribute of lore from the birds. A narrow green hollow, wedging itself into one of the gorges of the towering Peak, and watered by a snow-fed mountain brook, proved a very paradise for birds. Here was that queer little midget of the Rockies, the broad-tailed humming-bird, which performs such wonderful feats of balancing in the air; the red-shafted flicker; the western robin, singing precisely like his eastern half-brother; a pair of house-wrens guarding their treasures; Lincoln's sparrows, not quite so shy as those at Moraine Lake; mountain chickadees; olive-sided flycatchers; on the pine-clad mountain sides the lyrical hermit thrushes; and finally those ballad-singers of the mountain vales, the white-crowned sparrows, one of whose nests I was so fortunate as to come upon. It was placed in a small pine bush, and was just in process of construction. One of the birds flew fiercely at a mischievous chipmunk, and drove him away, as if he knew him for an arrant nest-robber.

Leaving this enchanting spot, I trudged down the mountain valleys and ravines, holding silent converse everywhere with the birds, and at length reached a small park, green and bushy, a short distance above the Halfway House. While jogging along, my eye caught sight of a gray-headed junco, which flitted from a clump of bushes bordering the stream to a spot on the ground close to some shrubs. The act appeared so suggestive that I decided to reconnoitre. I walked cautiously to the spot where the bird had dropped down, and in a moment she flew up with a scolding chipper. There was the nest, set on the ground in the grass and cosily hidden beneath the over-arching branches of a low bush.

Had the mother bird been wise and courageous enough to retain her place, her secret would not have been betrayed, the nest was so well concealed.

The pretty couch contained four juvenile juncos covered only with down, and yet, in spite of their extreme youth, their foreheads and lores showed black, and their backs a distinctly reddish tint, so early in life were they adopting the pattern worn by their parents. The persistency of species in the floral and faunal realms presents some hard nuts for the evolutionist to crack. But that is an excursus, and would lead us too far afield. This was the first junco's nest I had ever found, and no one can blame me for feeling gratified with the discovery. The gray-headed juncos were very abundant in the Rockies, and are the only species at present known to breed in the State of Colorado. They are differentiated from the common slate-colored snowbird by their ash-gray suits, modestly decorated with a rust-colored patch on the back.

It was now far past noon, and beginning to feel weak with hunger, I reluctantly said adieu to the junco and her brood, and hurried on to the Halfway House, where a luncheon of sandwiches, pie and coffee strengthened me for the remainder of my tramp down the mountain to Manitou. That was a walk which lingers like a Greek legend in my memory on account of--well, that is the story that remains to be told.

On a former visit to the Halfway House I was mentally knocked off my feet by several glimpses of a woodpecker which was entirely new to me, and of whose existence I was not even aware until this gorgeous gentleman hove in sight. He was the handsomest member of the Picid family I have ever seen--his upper parts glossy black, some portions showing a bluish iridescence; his belly rich sulphur yellow, a bright red median stripe on the throat, set in the midst of the black, looking like a small necktie; two white stripes running along the side of the head, and a large white patch covering the middle and greater wing-coverts. Altogether, an odd livery for a woodpecker. Silently he swung from bole to bole for a few minutes, and then disappeared.

Not until I reached my room in Manitou could I fix the bird's place in the avicular system. By consulting Coues's Key and Professor Cooke's brochure on the Birds of Colorado, I found this quaintly costumed woodpecker to be Williamson's sapsucker (Sphyrapicus thyroideus), known only in the western part of the United States from the Rocky Mountains to the Pacific coast. I now lingered in the beautiful pine grove surrounding the Halfway House, hoping to see him again, but he did not appear, and I reluctantly started down the cog-wheel track.

As I was turning a bend in the road, I caught sight of a mountain chickadee flitting to a dead snag on the slope at the right, the next moment slipping into a small hole leading inside. I climbed up to the shelf, a small level nook among the tall pines on the mountain side, to inspect her retreat, for it was the first nest of this interesting species that I found. The chickadee flashed in and out of the orifice, carrying food to her little ones, surreptitiously executing her housewifely duties. The mountain tit seems to be a shy and quiet little body when compared with the common black-cap known in the East.

While watching this bird from my place of concealment, I became conscious of the half-suppressed chirping of a woodpecker, and, to my intense joy, a moment later a Williamson's sapsucker swung to a pine bole a little below me and began pecking leisurely and with assumed nonchalance for grubs in the fissures of the bark. From my hiding-place behind some bushes I kept my eye on the handsome creature. An artist might well covet the privilege of painting this elegant bird as he scales the wall of a pine tree.

Presently he glided to a snag not more than a rod from the chickadee's domicile, and then I noticed that the dead bole was perforated by a number of woodpecker holes, into one of which the sapsucker presently slipped with the tidbit he held in his bill. The doorway was almost too small for him, obliging him to turn slightly sidewise and make some effort to effect an entrance. Fortune had treated me as one of her favorites: I had discovered the nest of Williamson's sapsucker.

But still another surprise was in store. A low, dubious chirping was heard, and then the female ambled leisurely to the snag and hitched up to the orifice. She made several efforts to enter, but could not while her spouse was within. Presently he wormed himself out, whereupon she went in, and remained for some time. At length I crept to the snag and beat against it with my cane. She was loath to leave the nest, but after a little while decided that discretion was the better part of valor. When she came out, my presence so near her nursery caused her not a little agitation, which she displayed by flinging about from bole to bole and uttering a nervous chirp.

As to costume, the male and the female had little in common. Her back was picturesquely mottled and barred with black and white, her head light brown, her breast decorated with a large black patch, and her other under parts yellow. Had the couple not been seen together flitting about the nest, they would not have been regarded as mates, so differently were they habited.

Standing before the doorway of the nursery--it was not quite so high as my head--I could plainly hear the chirping of the youngsters within. Much as I coveted the sight of a brood of this rare species, I could not bring myself to break down the walls of their cottage and thus expose them to the claws and beaks of their foes. Even scientific curiosity must be restrained by considerations of mercy.

The liege lord of the family had now disappeared. Desirous of seeing him once more, I hid myself in a bush-clump near at hand and awaited his return. Presently he came ambling along and scrambled into the orifice, turning his body sidewise, as he had done before. I made my way quietly to the snag and tapped upon it with my cane, but he did not come out, as I expected him to do. Then I struck the snag more vigorously. No result. Then I whacked the bole directly in the rear of the nest, while I stood close at one side watching the doorway. The bird came to the orifice, peeped out, then, seeing me, quickly drew back, determined not to desert his brood in what he must have regarded as an emergency. In spite of all my pounding and coaxing and feigned scolding--and I kept up the racket for several minutes--I did not succeed in driving the pater familias from his post of duty. Once he apparently made a slight effort to escape, but evidently stuck fast in the entrance, and so dropped back and would not leave, only springing up to the door and peeping out at me when my appeals became especially vigorous. It appeared like a genuine case of "I'm determined to defend my children, or die in the attempt!"

Meanwhile the mother bird was flitting about in an agitated way, uttering piteous cries of remonstrance and entreaty. Did that bandit intend to rob her of both her husband and her children? It was useless, if not wanton, to hector the poor creatures any longer, even to study their behavior under trying circumstances; and I left them in peace, and hurried down to my lodgings in Manitou, satisfied with the results of my day's ramble.

BIRDS OF THE ARID PLAIN

Having explored the summit of Pike's Peak and part of its southern slope down to the timber-line, and spent several delightful days in the upper valleys of the mountains, as well as in exploring several canyons, the rambler was desirous of knowing what species of birds reside on the plain stretching eastward from the bases of the towering ranges. One afternoon in the latter part of June, I found myself in a straggling village about forty miles east of Colorado Springs.

On looking around, I was discouraged, and almost wished I had not come; for all about me extended the parched and treeless plain, with only here and there a spot that had a cast of verdure, and even that was of a dull and sickly hue. Far off to the northeast rose a range of low hills sparsely covered with scraggy pines, but they were at least ten miles away, perhaps twenty, and had almost as arid an aspect as that of the plains themselves. Only one small cluster of deciduous trees was visible, about a mile up a shallow valley or "draw." Surely this was a most unpromising field for bird study. If I had only been content to remain among the mountains, where, even though the climbing was difficult, there were brawling brooks, shady woodlands, and green, copsy vales in which many feathered friends had lurked!

But wherever the bird-lover chances to be, his mania leads him to look for his favorites, and he is seldom disappointed; rather, he is often delightfully surprised. People were able to make a livelihood here, as was proved by the presence of the village and a few scattering dwellings on the plain; then why not the birds, which are as thrifty and wise in many ways as their human relatives? In a short time my baggage was stowed in a safe place, and, field-glass in hand, I sallied forth for my first jaunt on a Colorado plain. But, hold! what were these active little birds, hopping about on the street and sipping from the pool by the village well? They were the desert horned larks, so called because they select the dry plains of the West as their dwelling place. They are interesting birds. The fewer trees and the less humidity, provided there is a spot not too far away at which they may quench their thirst and rinse their feathers, the better they seem to be pleased. They were plentiful in this parched region, running or flying cheerfully before me wherever my steps were bent. I could not help wondering how many thousands of them--and millions, perhaps--had taken up free homesteads on the seemingly limitless plains of eastern Colorado.

Most of the young had already left the nest, and were flying about in the company of their elders, learning the fine art of making a living for themselves and evading the many dangers to which bird flesh is heir. The youngsters could readily be distinguished from their seniors by the absence of distinct black markings on throat, chest, and forehead, and the lighter cast of their entire plumage.

Sometimes these birds are called shore larks; but that is evidently a misnomer, or at least a very inapt name, for they are not in the least partial to the sea-shore or even the shores of lakes, but are more disposed to take up their residence in inland and comparatively dry regions. There are several varieties, all bearing a very close resemblance, so close, indeed, that only an expert ornithologist can distinguish them, even with the birds in hand. The common horned lark is well known in the eastern part of the United States as a winter resident, while in the middle West, Missouri, Kansas, Nebraska, etc., are to be found the prairie horned larks, which, as their name indicates, choose the open prairie for their home. The desert horned larks are tenants exclusively of the arid plains, mesas, and mountain parks of the West. There is still another variety, called the pallid horned lark, which spends the winter in Colorado, then hies himself farther north in summer to rear his brood.

As I pursued my walk, one of these birds suddenly assumed an alert attitude, then darted into the air, mounting up, up, up, in a series of swift leaps, like "an embodied joy whose race has just begun." Up he soared until he could no longer be seen with the naked eye, and even through my field-glass he was a mere speck against the blue canopy, and yet, high as he had gone, his ditty filtered down to me through the still, rarefied atmosphere, like a sifting of fine sand. His descent was a grand plunge, made with the swiftness of an Indian's arrow, his head bent downward, his wings partly folded, and his tail perked upward at precisely the proper angle to make a rudder, all the various organs so finely adjusted as to convert him into a perfectly dirigible parachute. Swift as his descent was, he alighted on the ground as lightly as a tuft of down. It was the poetry of motion. One or two writers have insisted that the horned lark's empyrean song compares favorably with that of the European skylark; but, loyal and patriotic an American as we are, honesty compels us to concede that our bird's voice is much feebler and less musical than that of his celebrated relative across the sea. It sounds like the unmelodious clicking of pebbles, while the song of the skylark is loud, clear, and ringing.

Our birds of the plain find insects to their taste in the short grass which carpets the land with greenish or olive gray. The following morning a mother lark was seen gathering insects and holding them in her bill--a sure sign of fledglings in the near neighborhood. I decided to watch her, and, if possible, find her bantlings. It required not a little patience, for she was wary and the sun poured down a flood of almost blistering heat. This way and that she scurried over the ground, now picking up an insect and adding it to the store already in her bill, and now standing almost erect to eye me narrowly and with some suspicion. At length she seemed to settle down for a moment upon a particular spot, and when I looked again with my glass, her beak was empty. I examined every inch of ground, as I thought, in the neighborhood of the place where she had stopped, but could find neither nest nor nestlings.

Again I turned my attention to the mother bird, which meanwhile had gathered another bunch of insects and was hopping about with them through the croppy grass, now and then adding to her accumulation until her mouth was full. For a long time she zigzagged about, going by provoking fits and starts. At length fortune favored me, for through my leveled glass I suddenly caught sight of a small, grayish-looking ball hopping and tumbling from a cactus clump toward the mother bird, who jabbed the contents of her bill into a small, open mouth. I followed a bee-line to the spot, and actually had to scan the ground sharply for a few moments before I could distinguish the youngster from its surroundings, for it had squatted flat, its gray and white plumage harmonizing perfectly with the grayish desert grass.

It was a dear little thing, and did not try to escape, although I took it up in my hand and stroked its downy back again and again. Sometimes it closed its eyes as if it were sleepy. When I placed it on the ground, it hopped away a few inches, and by accident punctured the fleshy corner of its mouth with a sharp cactus thorn, and had to jerk itself loose, bringing the blood from the lacerated part. Meanwhile the mother lark went calmly about her household duties, merely keeping a watchful eye on the human meddler, and making no outcry when she saw her infant in my possession. I may have been persona non grata, but, if so, she did not express her feeling. This was the youngest horned lark seen by me in my rambles on the plains.

Perhaps the reader will care to know something about the winter habits of these birds. They do not spend the season of cold and storm in the mountains, not even those that breed there, for the snow is very deep and the tempests especially fierce. Many of them, however, remain in the foothills and on the mesas and plains, where they find plenty of seeds and berries for their sustenance, unless the weather chances to be unusually severe. One winter, not long ago, the snow continued to lie much longer than usual, cutting off the natural food supply of the larks. What regimen did they adopt in that exigency? They simply went to town. Many of the kindly disposed citizens of Colorado Springs scattered crumbs and millet seeds on the streets and lawns, and of this supply the little visitors ate greedily, becoming quite tame. As soon, however, as the snow disappeared they took their departure, not even stopping to say thanks or adieu; although we may take it for granted that they felt grateful for favors bestowed.

Besides the horned larks, many other birds were found on the plain. Next in abundance were the western meadow-larks. Persons who live in the East and are familiar with the songs of the common meadow-lark, should hear the vocal performances of the westerners. The first time I heard one of them, the minstrelsy was so strange to my ear, so different from anything I had ever heard, I was thrown into an ecstasy of delight, and could not imagine from what kind of bird larynx so quaint a medley could emanate. The song opened with a loud, fine, piercing whistle, and ended with an abrupt staccato gurgle much lower in the musical staff, sounding precisely as if the soloist's performance had been suddenly choked off by the rising of water in the windpipe. It was something after the order of the purple martin's melodious sputter, only the tones were richer and fuller and the music better defined, as became a genuine oscine. His sudden and emphatic cessation seemed to indicate that he was in a petulant mood, perhaps impatient with the intruder, or angry with a rival songster.

Afterwards I heard him--or, rather, one of his brothers--sing arias so surpassingly sweet that I voted him the master minstrel of the western plains, prairies, and meadows. One evening as I was returning to Colorado Springs from a long tramp through one of the canyons of the mountains, a western meadow-lark sat on a small tree and sang six different tunes within the space of a few minutes. Two of them were so exquisite and unique that I involuntarily sprang to my feet with a cry of delight. There he sat in the lengthening shadows of Cheyenne Mountain, the champion phrase-fluter of the irrigated meadow in which he and a number of his comrades had found a summer home.

On the plain, at the time of my visit, the meadow-larks were not quite so tuneful, for here the seasons are somewhat earlier than in the proximity of the mountains, and the time of courtship and incubation was over. Still, they sang enough to prove themselves members of a gifted musical family. Observers in the East will remember the sputtering call of the eastern larks when they are alarmed or their suspicions are aroused. The western larks do not utter alarums of that kind, but a harsh "chack" instead, very similar to the call of the grackles. The nesting habits of the eastern and western species are the same, their domiciles being placed on the ground amid the grass, often prettily arched over in the rear and made snug and neat.

It must not be thought, because my monograph on the western larks is included in this chapter, that they dwell exclusively on the arid plain. No; they revel likewise in the areas of verdure bordering the streams, in the irrigated fields and meadows, and in the watered portions of the upper mountain parks.

An interesting question is the following: Are the eastern and western meadow-larks distinct species, or only varieties somewhat specialized by differences of locality and environment? It is a problem over which the scientific professors have had not a little disputation. My own opinion is that they are distinct species and do not cohabit, and the conviction is based on some special investigations, though not of the kind that are made with the birds in hand. It has been my privilege to study both forms in the field. In the first place, their vocal exhibitions are very different, so much so as to indicate a marked diversity in the organic structure of their larynxes. Much as I have listened to their minstrelsy, I have never known one kind to borrow from the musical repertory of the other. True, there are strains in the arias of the westerners that closely resemble the clear, liquid whistle of the eastern larks, but they occur right in the midst of the song and are part and parcel of it, and therefore afford no evidence of mimicry or amalgamation. Even the trills of the grassfinch and the song-sparrow have points of similarity; does that prove that they borrow from each other, or that espousals sometimes occur between the two species?

The habiliments of the two forms of larks are more divergent than would appear at first blush. Above, the coloration of neglecta (the western) is paler and grayer than that of magna, the black markings being less conspicuous, and those on the tertials and middle tail-feathers being arranged in narrow, isolated bars, and not connected along the shaft. While the flanks and under tail-coverts of magna are distinctly washed with buff, those of neglecta are white, very faintly tinged with buff, if at all. The yellow of the throat of the eastern form does not spread out laterally over the malar region, as does that of the western lark. All of which tends to prove that the two forms are distinct.

Early in the spring of 1901 the writer took a trip to Oklahoma in the interest of bird-study, and found both kinds of meadow-larks extremely abundant and lavish of their melodies on the fertile prairies. He decided to carry on a little original investigation in the field of inquiry now under discussion. One day, in a draw of the prairie, he noticed a western meadow-lark which was unusually lyrical, having the skill of a past-master in the art of trilling and gurgling and fluting. Again and again I went to the place, on the same day and on different days, and invariably found the westerner there, perching on the fence or a weed-stem, and greeting me with his exultant lays. But, mark: no eastern lark ever intruded on his preserve. In other and more distant parts of the broad field the easterners were blowing their piccolos, but they did not encroach on the domain of the lyrical westerner, who, with his mate--now on her nest in the grass--had evidently jumped his claim and held it with a high hand. In many other places in Oklahoma and Kansas where both species dwell, I have noticed the same interesting fact-- that in the breeding season each form selects a special precinct, into which the other form does not intrude. They perhaps put up some kind of trespass sign. These observations have all but convinced me that S. magna and S. neglecta are distinct species, and avoid getting mixed up in their family affairs.

Nor is that all. While both forms dwell on the vast prairies of Oklahoma, Kansas, and Nebraska, yet, as you travel eastward, the western larks gradually diminish in number until at length they entirely disappear; whereas, if you journey westward, the precise opposite occurs. I have never heard neglecta east of the Missouri River,[4] nor magna on the plains of Colorado. Therefore the conclusion is almost forced upon the observer that there are structural and organic differences between the two forms.

[4] He sometimes ventures, though sparingly, as far east as Illinois and Wisconsin; still my statement is true--I have never heard the western lark even in the bottoms and meadows of the broad valley east of the Missouri River, while, one spring morning, I did hear one of these birds fluting in the top of a cottonwood tree in my yard on the high western bluff of that stream.

After the foregoing deductions had been reached, the writer bethought him of consulting Ridgway's Manual on the subject, and was gratified to find his views corroborated by a footnote answering to an asterisk affixed to the name of the western lark:

"Without much doubt a distinct species. The occurrence of both S. neglecta and S. magna together in many portions of the Mississippi

Valley, each in its typical style (the ranges of the two overlapping, in fact, for a distance of several hundred miles), taken together with the excessive rarity of intermediate specimens and the universally attested radical difference in their notes, are facts wholly incompatible with the theory of their being merely geographical races of the same species."

This has been a long excursus, and we must get back to our jaunt on the plain. While I was engaged in watching the birds already named, my ear was greeted by a loud, clear, bell-like call; and, on looking in the direction from which it came, I observed a bird hovering over a ploughed field not far away, and then descending with graceful, poising flight to the ground. It proved to be the Arkansas flycatcher, a large, elegant bird that is restricted to the West. I had never seen this species. Nothing like him is known in the East, the crested flycatcher being most nearly a copy of him, although the manners of the two birds are quite unlike. The body of the western bird is as large as that of the robin, and he must be considerably longer from tip of beak to tip of tail. He is a fine-looking fellow, presenting a handsome picture as he stands on a weed-stalk or a fence-post, his yellow jacket gleaming in the sun. He is the possessor of a clear, musical voice, and if he had the vocal organs of some of the oscines, he certainly would be one of the best feathered lyrists of America. Unfortunately he is able to do nothing but chirp and chatter, although he puts not a little music into his simple vocal exercises.

It was surprising to note on how slender a weed-stalk so large a bird was able to perch. There being few trees and fences in this region, he has doubtless gained expertness through practice in the art of securing a foot-hold on the tops of the weed-stems. Some of the weeds on which he stood with perfect ease and grace were extremely lithe and flexible and almost devoid of branches.

But what was the cause of this particular bird's intense solicitude? It was obvious there was a nest in the neighborhood. As I sought in the grass and weed-clumps, he uttered his piercing calls of protest and circled and hovered overhead like a red-winged blackbird. Suddenly the thought occurred to me that the flycatchers of my acquaintance do not nest on the ground, but on trees. I looked around, and, sure enough, in the shallow hollow below me stood a solitary willow tree not more than fifteen or twenty feet high, the only tree to be seen within a mile. And that lone tree on the plain was occupied by the flycatcher and his mate for a nesting place. In a crotch the gray cottage was set, containing three callow babies and one beautifully mottled egg.

In another fork of the same small tree a pair of kingbirds--the same species as our well-known eastern bee-martins--had built their nest, in the downy cup of which lay four eggs similarly decorated with brown spots. The birds now all circled overhead and joined in an earnest plea with me not to destroy their homes and little ones, and I hurriedly climbed down from the tree to relieve their agitation, stopping only a moment to examine the twine plaited into the felted nests of the kingbirds. The willow sapling contained also the nest of a turtle dove.

"If there are three nests in this small tree, there may be a large number in the cluster of trees beyond the swell about a mile away," I mused, and forthwith made haste to go to the place indicated. I was not disappointed. Had the effort been made, I am sure two score of nests might have been found in these trees, for they were liberally decorated with bird cots and hammocks. Most of these were kingbirds' and Arkansas flycatchers' nests, but there were others as well. On one small limb there were four of the dangling nests of Bullock's orioles, one of them fresh, the rest more or less weather beaten, proving that this bird had been rearing broods here for a number of seasons.

Whose song was this ringing from one of the larger trees a little farther down the glade? I could scarcely believe the testimony of my ears and eyes, yet there could be no mistake--it was the vivacious mimicry of the mocking-bird, which had travelled far across the plain to this solitary clump of trees to find singing perches and a site for his nests. He piped his musical miscellany with as much good-cheer as if he were dwelling in the neighborhood of some embowered cottage in Dixie-land. In suitable localities on the plains of Colorado the mockers were found to be quite plentiful, but none were seen among the mountains.

A network of twigs and vines in one of the small willows afforded a support and partial covert for the nest of a pair of white-rumped shrikes. It contained six thickly speckled eggs, and was the first nest of this species I had ever found. The same hollow,--if so shallow a dip in the plain can be called a hollow,--was selected as the home of several pairs of red-winged and Brewer's blackbirds, which built their grassy cots in the low bushes of a slightly boggy spot, where a feeble spring oozed from the ground. It was a special pleasure to find a green-tailed towhee in the copse of the draw, for I had supposed that he always hugged close to the steep mountain sides.

A walk before breakfast the next morning added several more avian species to my roll. To my surprise, a pair of mountain bluebirds had chosen the village for their summer residence, and were building a nest in the coupler of a freight car standing on a side track. The domicile was almost completed, and I could not help feeling sorry for the pretty, innocent couple, at the thought that the car would soon be rolling hundreds of miles away, and all their loving toil would go for naught. Bluebirds had previously been seen at the timber-line among the mountains, and here was a pair forty miles out on the plain--quite a range for this species, both longitudinally and vertically.

During the forenoon the following birds were observed: A family of juvenile Arkansas flycatchers, which were being fed by their parents; a half-dozen or more western grassfinches, trilling the same pensive tunes as their eastern half-brothers; a small, long-tailed sparrow, which I could not identify at the time, but which I now feel certain was Lincoln's sparrow; these, with a large marsh-harrier and a colony of cliff-swallows, completed my bird catalogue at this place. It may not be amiss to add that several jack-rabbits went skipping over the swells; that many families of prairie dogs were visited, and that a coyotte galloped lightly across the plain, stopping and looking back occasionally to see whether he were being pursued.

It was no difficult task to study the birds on the plain. Having few hiding-places in a locality almost destitute of trees and bushes, where even the grass was too short to afford a covert, they naturally felt little fear of man, and hence were easily approached. Their cousins residing in the mountains were, as a rule, provokingly wary. The number of birds that had pre-empted homesteads on the treeless wastes was indeed a gratifying surprise, and I went back to the mountains refreshed by the pleasant change my brief excursion upon the plains had afforded me.

A PRETTY HUMMER

Where do you suppose I got my first glimpse of the mite in feathers called the broad-tailed humming-bird? It was in a green bower in the Rocky Mountains in plain sight of the towering summit of Pike's Peak, which seemed almost to be standing guard over the place. Two brawling mountain brooks met here, and, joining their forces, went with increased speed and gurgle down the glades and gorges. As they sped through this ravine, they slightly overflowed their banks, making a boggy area of about an acre as green as green could be; and here amid the grass and bushes a number of birds found a pleasant summer home, among them the dainty hummer.

From the snow-drifts, still to be seen in the sheltered gorges of Pike's Peak, the breezes would frequently blow down into the nook with a freshness that stimulated like wine with no danger of intoxicating; and it was no wonder that the white-crowned sparrows, Lincoln's sparrows, the robins and wrens, and several other species, found in this spot a pleasant place to live. One of the narrow valleys led directly up to the base of the massive cone of the Peak, its stream fed by the snow-fields shining in the sun. Going around by the valley of Seven Lakes, I had walked down from the summit, but nowhere had I seen the tiny hummer until I reached the green nook just described. Still, he sometimes ascends to an elevation of eleven thousand feet above the level of the sea.

ONE OF THE SEVEN LAKES

PIKE'S PEAK shows dimly in the background, more plainly in the reflection. Viewed from the peak, the lakes sparkle like opaline gems in the sun. The waters are so clear that an inverted world is seen in their transparent depths. The valley is an elysium for many kinds of birds, most of them described in the text. The white-crowned sparrows love the shores of these beautiful lakes, which mirror the blithe forms of the birds. The pine forests of the mountain sides are vocal with the refrains of the hermit thrushes.

Our feathered dot is gorgeous with his metallic green upper parts, bordered on the tail with purplish black, his white or grayish under parts, and his gorget of purple which gleams in bright, varying tints in the sun. He closely resembles our common ruby-throated humming-bird, whose gorget is intense crimson instead of purple, and who does not venture into the Rocky Mountain region, but dwells exclusively in the eastern part of North America. It is a little strange that the eastern part of our country attracts only one species of the large hummer family, while the western portion, including the Rocky Mountain region, can boast of at least seventeen different kinds as summer residents or visitors.

My attention was first directed to the broad-tailed hummer by seeing him darting about in the air with the swiftness of an arrow, sipping honey from the flower cups, and then flying to the twigs of a dead tree that stood in the marsh. There he sat, turning his head this way and that, and watching me with his keen little eyes. It was plain he did not trust me, and therefore resented my presence. Though an unwelcome guest, I prolonged my call for several hours, during which I made many heroic but vain attempts to find his nest.

But what was the meaning of a sharp, insect-like buzzing that fell at intervals on my ear? Presently I succeeded in tracing the sound to the hummer, which utters it whenever he darts from his perch and back again, especially if there is a spectator or a rival near at hand, for whom he seems in this way to express his contempt. It is a vocal sound, or, at least, it comes from his throat, and is much louder and sharper than the susurrus produced by the rapid movement of his wings. This I ascertain by hearing both the sounds at the same time.

But the oddest prank which this hummer performs is to dart up in the air, and then down, almost striking a bush or a clump of grass at each descent, repeating this feat a number of times with a swiftness that the eye can scarcely follow. Having done this, he will swing up into the air so far that you can scarcely see him with the naked eye; the next moment he will drop into view, poise in mid-air seventy-five or a hundred feet above your head, supporting himself by a swift motion of the wings, and simply hitching to right and left in short arcs, as if he were fixed on a pivot, sometimes meanwhile whirling clear around. There he hangs on his invisible axis until you grow tired watching him, and then he darts to his favorite perch on the dead tree.

No doubt John Vance Cheney had in mind another species when he composed the following metrical description, but it aptly characterized the volatile broad-tail as well:

"Voyager on golden air, Type of all that's fleet and fair, Incarnate gem, Live diadem, Bird-beam of the summer day,-- Whither on your sunny way?

* * * * *

Stay, forget lost Paradise, Star-bird fallen from happy skies."

After that first meeting the broad-tailed hummers were frequently seen in my rambles among the Rockies. In some places there were small colonies of them. They did not always dwell together in harmony, but often pursued one another like tiny furies, with a loud z-z-z-zip that meant defiance and war. The swiftness of their movements often excited my wonder, and it was difficult to see how they kept from impaling themselves on thorns or snags, so reckless were their lightning-like passages through the bushes and trees. When four or five of them were found in one place, they would fairly thread the air with green and purple as they described their circles and loops and festoons with a rapidity that fairly made my head whirl. At one place several of them grew very bold, dashing at me or wheeling around my head, coming so close that I could hear the susurrus of their wings as well as the sharp, challenging buzz from their throats.

Perhaps it would interest you to know where the rambler found these tiny hummers. They were never in the dark canyons and gorges, nor in the ravines that were heavily wooded with pine, but in the open, sunshiny glades and valleys, where there were green grass and bright flowers. In the upper part of both North and South Cheyenne Canyons they were plentiful, although they avoided the most scenic parts of these wonderful mountain gorges. Another place where they found a pleasant summer home was in a green pocket of the mountain above Red Cliff, a village on the western side of the great range. On descending the mountains to the town of Glenwood, I did not find them, and therefore am disposed to think that in the breeding season they do not choose to dwell in too low or too high an altitude, but seek suitable places at an elevation of from seven thousand to nine thousand feet.

SUMMIT OF PIKE'S PEAK

Only a small portion of the peak is shown in the view. The comparatively level area referred to in the text lies back of the signal station on the crest. At a garbage heap near the building a flock of leucostictes were seen, and the writer was told that they came there regularly to feed. From this sublime height the American pipits rise on resilient wings hundreds of feet into the air until they disappear in the cerulean depths of the sky, singing all the while at "heaven's gate."

One day, while staying at Buena Vista, Colorado, I hired a saddle-horse and rode to Cottonwood Lake, twelve miles away, among the rugged mountains. The valley is wide enough here to admit of a good deal of sunshine, and therefore flowers studded the ground in places. It was here I saw the only female broad-tailed hummer that was met with in my rambles in the Rockies. She was flitting among the flowers, and did not make the buzzing sound that the males produce wherever found. She was not clad so elegantly as were her masculine relatives, for the throat-patch was white instead of purple, and the green on her back did not gleam so brightly. But, oddly enough, her sides and under tail-coverts were stained with a rufous tint--a color that does not appear at all in the costume of the male.

A curious habit of these hummers is worth describing. The males remain in the breeding haunts until the young are out of the nest and are beginning to be able to shift for themselves. Then the papas begin to disappear, and in about ten days all have gone, leaving the mothers and the youngsters to tarry about the summer home until the latter are strong enough to make the journey to some resort lower in the mountains or farther south. The reason the males do this is perhaps evident enough, for at a certain date the flowers upon whose sweets the birds largely subsist begin to grow scant, and so if they remained there would not be enough for all.

In the San Francisco Mountains of Arizona, Doctor Merriam found the broad-tails very abundant in the balsam timber and the upper part of the pine belt, where they breed in the latter part of July; after which they remain in that region until the middle of September, even though the weather often becomes quite frosty at night. At break of day, in spite of the cold, they will gather in large flocks at some spring to drink and bathe. Doctor Merriam says about them at such times:

"They were like swarms of bees, buzzing about one's head and darting to and fro in every direction. The air was full of them. They would drop down to the water, dip their feet and bellies, and rise and shoot away as if propelled by an unseen power. They would often dart at the face of an intruder as if bent on piercing the eye with their needle-like bills, and then poise for a moment almost within reach before turning, when they were again lost in the busy throng. Whether this act was prompted by curiosity or resentment I was not able to ascertain."

As has already been said, there is not always unruffled peace in the hummer family. Among the Rocky Mountains, and especially on the western side of the range, there dwells another little hummer called the rufous humming-bird, because the prevailing color of his plumage is reddish, and between this family and the broad-tails there exists a bitter feud. When, in the migrating season, a large number of both species gather together in a locality where there is a cluster of wild-flowers, the picture they make as they dart to and fro and bicker and fight for some choice blossom, their metallic colors flashing in the sun, is so brilliant as never to be forgotten by the spectator who is fortunate enough to witness it.

OVER THE DIVIDE AND BACK

One June day a Denver & Rio Grande train bore the bird-lover from Colorado Springs to Pueblo, thence westward to the mountains, up the Grand Canyon of the Arkansas River, through the Royal Gorge, past the smiling, sunshiny upper mountain valleys, over the Divide at Tennessee Pass, and then down the western slopes to the next stopping-place, which was Red Cliff, a village nestling in a deep mountain ravine at the junction of Eagle River and Turkey Creek. The following day, a little after "peep o' dawn," I was out on the street, and was impressed by a song coming from the trees on the acclivity above the village. "Surely that is a new song," I said to myself; "and yet it seems to have a familiar air." A few minutes of hard climbing brought me near enough to get my glass on the little lyrist, and then I found it was only the house-wren! "How could you be led astray by so familiar a song?" you inquire. Well, that is the humiliating part of the incident, for I have been listening to the house-wren's gurgling sonata for some twenty years--rather more than less--and should have recognized it at once; only it must be remembered that I was in a strange place, and had my ears and eyes set for avian rarities, and therefore blundered.[5]

[5] On this incident I quote a personal note from my friend, Mr. Aiken: "The wren of the Rockies is the western house-wren, but is the same form as that found in the Mississippi Valley. It is quite possible that a difference in song may occur, but I have not noticed any."

To my surprise, I found many birds on those steep mountain sides, which were quite well timbered. Above the village a colony of cliff-swallows had a nesting place on the rugged face of a cliff, and were soaring about catching insects and attending to the wants of their greedy young.

Besides the species named, I here found warbling vireos, broad-tailed humming-birds, western nighthawks, ruby-crowned kinglets, magpies, summer warblers, mountain chickadees, western wood-pewees, Louisiana tanagers, long-crested jays, kingfishers, gray-headed juncos, red-shafted flickers, pygmy nuthatches, house-finches, mountain jays, and Clarke's nutcrackers. The only species noted here that had not previously been seen east of the Divide was the pygmy nuthatch, a little bird which scales the trunks and branches of trees like all his family, but which is restricted to the Rocky Mountains. Like the white-breasted nuthatch, he utters an alto call, "Yang! yang! yang!" only it is soft and low--a miniature edition of the call of its eastern relative.

A mountain chickadee's nest was also found, and here I heard for the first time one of these birds sing. Its performance was quite an affecting little minor whistle, usually composed of four distinct notes, though sometimes the vocalist contented himself with a song of two or three syllables. The ordinary run might be represented phonetically in this way, "Phee, ph-e-e-e, phe-phe," with the chief emphasis on the second syllable, which is considerably prolonged. The song is quite different from that of the black-capped chickadee both in the intoning and the technical arrangement, while it does not run so high in the scale, nor does it impress me as being quite so much of a minor strain, if such a distinction can be made in music. Both birds' tunes, however, have the character of being whistled.

Glenwood is a charming summer resort in Colorado on the western side of the Rocky Mountain range, and can be reached by both the Denver & Rio Grande and the Colorado Midland Railways. Beautifully situated in an open mountain valley, it possesses many attractions in the way of natural scenery, while the cool breezes blow down from the snow-mantled ranges gleaming in the distance, and the medicinal springs draw many tourists in search of health and recuperation.

My purpose, however, in visiting this idyllic spot--I went there from Red Cliff--was not primarily to view the scenery, nor to make use of the healing waters, but to gratify my thirst for bird-lore. Having spent some weeks in observing the avi-fauna east of the range, I had a curiosity to know something of bird life west of the great chain of alpine heights, and therefore I selected Glenwood as a fertile field in which to carry on some investigations. While my stay at this resort was all too short, it was of sufficient length to put me in possession of a number of facts that may prove to be of general interest.

For one thing I learned, somewhat to my surprise, that the avian fauna on both sides of the Divide is much the same. Indeed, with one exception--to be noted more at length hereafter--I found no birds on the western side that I had not previously seen on the eastern side, although a longer and minuter examination would undoubtedly have resulted in the discovery of a few species that are peculiar to the regions beyond the range. In the extreme western and southwestern portions of Colorado there are quite a number of species that are seldom or never seen in the eastern part of the State. However, keeping to the mountainous districts, and given the same altitude and other conditions, you will be likely to find the same kinds of feathered folk on both sides of the range. A few concrete cases will make this statement clear. The elevation of Glenwood is five thousand seven hundred and fifty-eight feet; that of Colorado Springs, five thousand nine hundred and ninety-two feet; and the climatic conditions otherwise are practically the same. Hence at both places the following species were found: Lazuli buntings, Arkansas goldfinches, American goldfinches, western wood-pewees, Arkansas kingbirds, Bullock's orioles, grassfinches, and catbirds. At the same time there were a number of species in both localities that have a more extensive vertical range, as, for example, the western robins, which were seen in many places from the bases of the mountains up to the timber-line, over eleven thousand five hundred feet above sea-level.

ROYAL GORGE

In the Grand Canyon of the Arkansas River. In canyons like this, their walls rising almost vertically from one thousand to fifteen hundred feet, few birds are to be seen. Occasionally a dove will fly from one side of the gorge to the other before the scurrying train. From below a magpie or a Clark's crow may sometimes be seen flying overhead across the fearful chasm from one wall to the other, turning its head at intervals as if to inspect and question the spectator over a thousand feet below.

The presence of practically the same avian fauna on both sides of the great range suggests some speculations as to their movements in the migrating season. Do those on the western side of the mountains travel over the towering summits from the eastern plains? Or do they come up from their southern winter homes by way of the valleys and plains west of the range? Undoubtedly the latter is the correct surmise, for there were birds at Glenwood that are never known to ascend far into the mountains, and should they attempt to cross the Divide in the early spring, they would surely perish in the intense cold of those elevated regions, where snow often falls even in June, July, and August. One can easily imagine some of the eastern and western residents meeting in the autumn on the plains at the southern extremity of the mountain range, dwelling together in some southern locality throughout the winter, and then, when spring approaches, taking their separate routes, part going east and part west of the range, for their breeding haunts in the North. More than likely they do not meet again until the following autumn. There are individuals, doubtless, that never catch a glimpse of the western side of the great American watershed, while others are deprived of the privilege of looking upon the majestic panoramas of the eastern side.

What has just been said applies, of course, only to those species that prefer to dwell in the lower altitudes. There are other species that find habitats to their taste in the most elevated localities, ranging at will in the summer time over the bald summits in the regions of perpetual snow. Among these may be mentioned the brown-capped leucostictes, the American pipits, the ravens, and Brewer's blackbirds. These species will often have the privilege of looking upon the scenery on both sides of the range, and you and I can scarcely repress a feeling of envy when we think of their happy freedom, and their frequent opportunities to go sightseeing.

While taking an early morning stroll along one of the streets of Glenwood, I caught sight of a new member of the phoebe family, its reddish breast and sides differentiating it from the familiar phoebe of the East. Afterwards I identified it as Say's phoebe, a distinctly western species. Its habits are like those of its eastern relative. A pair of Say's phoebes had placed their nest on a beam of a veranda, near the roof, where they could be seen carrying food to their young. My notes say nothing of their singing a tune or even uttering a chirp. This was my first observation of Say's phoebe, although, as will be seen, I subsequently saw one under somewhat peculiar circumstances.

Having spent all the time I could spare at Glenwood, one morning I boarded the eastward-bound train, and was soon whirling up through the sublime canyons of Grand and Eagle Rivers, keeping on the alert for such birds as I could see from the car-window. Few birds, as has been said, can be seen in the dark gorges of the mountains, the species that are most frequently descried being the turtle doves, with now and then a small flock of blackbirds. The open, sunlit valleys of the upper mountains, watered by the brawling streams, are much more to the liking of many birds, especially the mountain song-sparrows, the white-crowned sparrows, the green-tailed towhees, and Audubon's and Wilson's warblers. Up, up, for many miles the double-headed train crept, tooting and puffing hard, until at length it reached the highest point on the route, which is Tennessee Pass, through the tunnel of which it swept with a sullen roar, issuing into daylight on the eastern side, where the waters of the streams flow eastward instead of westward. The elevation of this tunnel is ten thousand four hundred and eighteen feet, which is still about a thousand feet below the timber-line. A minute after emerging from the tunnel's mouth I caught sight of a red-shafted flicker which went bolting across the narrow valley. The train swept down the valley for some miles, stopped long enough to have another engine coupled to the one that had brought us down from the tunnel, then wheeled to the left and began the ascent to the city of Leadville. This city is situated on a sloping plain on the mountain side, in full view of many bald mountain peaks whose gorges are filled with deep snow-drifts throughout the summer. For some purposes Leadville may be an exceedingly desirable city, but it has few attractions for the ornithologist. I took a long walk through a part of the city, and, whether you will believe it or not, I did not see a single bird outside of a cage, not even a house-finch or an English sparrow, nor did I see one tree in my entire stroll along the busy streets. The caged birds seen were a canary and a cardinal, and, oddly enough, both of them were singing, mayhap for very homesickness.

Why should a bird student tarry here? What was there to keep him in a birdless place like this? I decided to leave at once, and so, checking my baggage through to Buena Vista, I started afoot down the mountain side, determined to walk to Malta, a station five miles below, observing the birds along the way. Not a feathered lilter was seen until I had gone about a mile from Leadville, when a disconsolate robin appeared among some scraggy pine bushes, not uttering so much as a chirp by way of greeting.

A few minutes later I heard a vigorous and musical chirping in the pine bushes, and, turning aside, found a flock of small, finch-like birds. They flitted about so rapidly that it was impossible to get a good view of them with my glasses; but such glimpses as I obtained revealed a prevailing grayish, streaked with some darker color, while a glint of yellow in their wings and tails was displayed as the birds flew from bush to bush. When the wings were spread, a narrow bar of yellow or whitish-yellow seemed to stretch across them lengthwise, giving them a gauzy appearance. The birds remained together in a more or less compact flock. They uttered a loud, clear chirp that was almost musical, and also piped a quaint trill that was almost as low and harsh as that of the little clay-colored sparrow, although occasionally one would lift his voice to a much higher pitch. What were these tenants of the dry and piney mountain side? They were pine siskins, which I had ample opportunity to study in my rambles among the mountains in 1901.

A mile farther down, a lone mountain bluebird appeared in sight, perched on a gray stump on the gray hillside, and keeping as silent as if it were a crime in bluebird-land to utter a sound. This bird's breeding range extends from the plains to the timber-line; and he dwells on both sides of the mountains, for I met with him at Glenwood. About a half mile above Malta a western nighthawk was seen, hurtling in his eccentric, zigzag flight overhead, uttering his strident call, and "hawking for flies," as White of Selborne would phrase it. A western grassfinch flew over to some bushes with a morsel in its bill, but I could not discover its nest or young, search as I would. Afterwards it perched on a telegraph wire and poured out its evening voluntary, which was the precise duplicate of the trills of the grassfinches of eastern North America. There seems to be only a slight difference between the eastern and western forms of these birds, so slight, indeed, that they can be distinguished only by having the birds in hand.

Turtle doves were also plentiful in the valley above Malta, as they were in most suitable localities. Here were also several western robins, one of which saluted me with a cheerful carol, whose tone and syllabling were exactly like those of the merry redbreast of our Eastern States. I was delighted to find the sweet-voiced white-crowned sparrows tenants of this valley, although they were not so abundant here as they had been a little over a week before in the hollows below the summit of Pike's Peak. But what was the bird which was singing so blithely a short distance up the slope? He remained hidden until I drew near, when he ran off on the ground like a frightened doe, and was soon ensconced in a sage bush. Note his chestnut crest and greenish back. This is the green-tailed towhee. He is one of the finest vocalists of the Rocky Mountains, his tones being strong and well modulated, his execution almost perfect as to technique, and his entire song characterized by a quality that might be defined as human expressiveness.

A pair of western chipping sparrows were feeding their young in one of the sage bushes. I hoped to find a nest, but my quest simply proved that the bantlings had already left their nurseries. It was some satisfaction, however, to establish the fact at first hand that the western chipping sparrows breed at an elevation of nine thousand five hundred and eighty feet above sea-level.

While strolling about a short distance above the town, I discovered an underground passage leading to some of the factories, or perhaps the smelting works, a few miles farther up the valley. The over-arching ground and timbers forming the roof were broken through at various places, making convenient openings for the unwary pedestrian to tumble through should he venture to stroll about here by night. Suddenly a little broad-shouldered bird appeared from some mysterious quarter, and flitted silently about from bush to bush or from one tussock of grass to another. To my surprise, he presently dropped into one of the openings of the subterranean passage, disappeared for a few moments, and then emerged from another opening a little farther away. The bird--let me say at once--was Say's phoebe, with which, as previously told, I made acquaintance at Glenwood. He may be recognized by the reddish or cinnamon-brown cast of his abdomen and sides. Again and again he darted into the passage, perhaps to make sure that his bairns had not been kidnapped, and then came up to keep a vigilant eye on his visitor, whom he was not wholly disposed to trust. I am not sure that there was a nest in the subterranean passage, as my time was too short to look for it. Others may not regard it as an important ornithological discovery, and I do not pretend that it was epoch-making, but to me it was at least interesting to find this species, which was new to me, dwelling at an elevation of five thousand seven hundred and fifty-eight feet on the western side of the range, and on the eastern side at an elevation of nine thousand five hundred and eighty feet. Nowhere else in my peregrinations among the Rockies did I so much as catch a glimpse of Say's phoebe.[6]

[6] In 1901 this bird was seen by me in South Park, and its quaint whistle was heard,--it says Phe-by, but its tone and expression are different from those of its eastern relative. See the chapter entitled "Pleasant Outings."

With the exception of some swallows circling about in the air, I saw no other birds during my brief stay at Malta. I was sorely disappointed in not being able to find accommodation at this place, for it had been my intention to remain here for the night, and walk the next day to a station called Granite, some seventeen miles farther down the valley, making observations on bird life in the region by the way. To this day I regret that my calculations went "agley"; but I was told that accommodation was not to be secured at Malta "for love or money," and so I shook the dust from my feet, and boarded an evening train for my next stopping-place, which was Buena Vista.

The elevation of this beautiful mountain town is seven thousand nine hundred and sixty-seven feet. It nestles amid cottonwood trees and green meadows in a wide valley or park, and is flanked on the east by the rolling and roaring Arkansas River, while to the west the plain slopes up gradually to the foothills of the three towering college peaks,--Harvard, Yale, and Princeton,--crowned all the year with snow. And here were birds in plenty. Before daybreak the avian concert began with the shrieking of the western wood-pewees--a vocal performance that they, in their innocence, seriously mistake for melody--and continued until night had again settled on the vale. In this place I spent three or four days, giving myself up to my favorite study and pastime, and a list of all the birds that I saw in the neighborhood would surprise the reader. However, a mere catalogue would be of slight interest, I apprehend, and therefore mention will be made only of those species which I had not seen elsewhere, passing by such familiar feathered folk as the Arkansas goldfinches, catbirds, western meadow-larks, Brewer's blackbirds, house-finches, green-tailed towhees, magpies, long-crested jays, summer warblers, and many others, begging their pardon, of course, for paying them such scant courtesy.

Early on a bright morning I was following one of the streets of the village, when, on reaching the suburbs, I was greeted by a blithe, dulcet trill which could come from no other vocalist than the song-sparrow. His tones and vocalization were precisely like those of Melospiza fasciata, to which I have so often listened in my native State of Ohio. It was a dulcet strain, and stirred memories half sad, half glad, of many a charming ramble about my eastern home when the song-sparrows were the chief choralists in the outdoor opera festival. Peering into the bushes that fringed the gurgling mountain brook, I soon caught sight of the little triller, and found that, so far as I could distinguish them with my field-glass, his markings were just like those of his eastern relative--the same mottled breast, with the large dusky blotch in the centre.

Delighted as I was with the bird's aria, I could not decide whether this was the common song-sparrow or the mountain song-sparrow. Something over a week earlier I had seen what I took to be the mountain song-sparrow in a green nook below the summit of Pike's Peak, and had noted his trill as a rather shabby performance in comparison with the tinkling chansons of the song-sparrow of the East. Had I mistaken some other bird for the mountain song-sparrow? Or was the Buena Vista bird the common song-sparrow which had gone entirely beyond its Colorado range? Consulting Professor W. W. Cooke's list of Colorado birds, I found that Melospiza fasciata is marked "migratory, rare," and has been known thus far only in the extreme eastern part of the State; whereas Melospiza fasciata montana is a summer resident, "common throughout the State in migration, and not uncommon as a breeder from the plains to eight thousand feet."

But Professor Cooke fails to give a clue to the song of either variety, and therefore my little problem remains unsolved, as I could not think of taking the life of a dulcet-voiced bird merely to discover whether it should have "montana" affixed to its scientific name or not. All I can say is, if this soloist was a mountain song-sparrow, he reproduced exactly the trills of his half-brothers of the East.[7] On the morning of my departure from Buena Vista another song-sparrow sang his matins, in loud, clear tones among the bushes of a stream that flowed through the town, ringing quite a number of changes in his tune, all of them familiar to my ear from long acquaintance with the eastern forms of the Melospiza subfamily.

[7] The problem has since been solved, through the aid of Mr. Aiken. The Buena Vista bird was montana, while the bird in the Pike's Peak hollow was Lincoln's sparrow.

How well I recall a rainy afternoon during my stay at Buena Vista! The rain was not so much of a downpour as to drive me indoors, although it made rambling in the bushes somewhat unpleasant. What was this haunting song that rose from a thick copse fringing one of the babbling mountain brooks? It mingled sweetly with the patter of the rain upon the leaves. Surely it was the song of the veery thrush! The same rich, melodious strain, sounding as if it were blown through a wind-harp, setting all the strings a-tune at the same time. Too long and closely had I studied the veery's minstrelsy in his summer haunts in northern Minnesota to be deceived now--unless, indeed, this fertile avian region produced another thrush which whistled precisely the same tune. The bird's alarm-call was also like that of the veery. The few glimpses he permitted of his flitting, shadowy form convinced me that he must be a veery, and so I entered him in my note-book.

But on looking up the matter--for the bird student must aim at accuracy--what was my surprise to find that the Colorado ornithologists have decided that the veery thrush is not a resident of the State, nor even an occasional visitor! Of course I could not set up my judgment against that of those scientific gentlemen. But what could this minstrel be? I wrote to my friend, Mr. Charles E. Aiken, of Colorado Springs, who replied that the bird was undoubtedly the willow thrush, which is the western representative of the veery. I am willing to abide by this decision, especially as Ridgway indicates in his Manual that there is very little difference in the coloration of the two varieties. One more mile-post had been passed in my never-ending ornithological journey--I had learned for myself and others that the willow thrush of the Rockies and the veery of our Eastern and Middle States have practically the same musical repertory, and nowhere in the East or the West is sweeter and more haunting avian minstrelsy to be heard, if only it did not give one that sad feeling which Heine calls Heimweh!

A ROCKY MOUNTAIN LAKE

"You will find a small lake just about a mile from town. Follow the road leading out this way"--indicating the direction--"until you come to a red gate. The lake is private property, but you can go right in, as you don't shoot. No one will drive you out. I think you will find it an interesting place for bird study."

The foregoing is what my landlord told me one morning at Buena Vista. Nor did I waste time in finding the way to the lake, a small sheet of water, as clear as crystal, embowered in the lovely park lying between towering, snow-clad mountains. One might almost call the spot a bird's Arcadia. In no place, in all my tramping among the Rockies, did I find so many birds in an equal area.

In the green, irrigated meadow bordering one side of the sheet of water, I was pleased to find a number of Brewer's blackbirds busily gathering food in the wet grass for their young. And who or what are Brewer's blackbirds? In the East, the purple and bronzed grackles, or crow blackbirds, are found in great abundance; but in Colorado these birds are replaced by Brewer's blackbirds, which closely resemble their eastern kinsfolk, although not quite so large. The iridescence of the plumage is somewhat different in the two species, but in both the golden eye-balls show white at a distance. When I first saw a couple of Brewer's blackbirds stalking featly about on a lawn at Manitou, digging worms and grubs out of the sod, I simply put them down in my note-book as bronzed or purple grackles--an error that had to be corrected afterwards, on more careful examination. The mistake shows how close is the resemblance between the two species.

The Brewer division of the family breed on the plains and in the mountains, to an altitude of ten thousand feet, always selecting marshy places for their early summer home; then in August and September, the breeding season over, large flocks of old and young ascend to the regions above the timber-line, about thirteen thousand feet above sea-level, where they swarm over the grassy but treeless mountain sides in search of food. In October they retire to the plains, in advance of the austere weather of the great altitudes, and soon the majority of them hie to a blander climate than Colorado affords in winter.

Still more interesting to me was the large colony of yellow-headed blackbirds that had taken up their residence in the rushes and flags of the upper end of the lake. These birds are not such exclusive westerners as their ebon-hued cousins just described; for I found them breeding at Lake Minnetonka, near Minneapolis, Minnesota, a few years ago, and they sometimes straggle, I believe, as far east as Ohio. A most beautiful bird is this member of the

Icterid family, a kind of Beau Brummel among his fellows, with his glossy black coat and rich yellow--and even orange, in highest feather--mantle covering the whole head, neck, and breast, and a large white, decorative spot on the wings, showing plainly in flight. He is the handsomest blackbird with which I am acquainted.

At the time of my visit to the lake, the latter part of June, the yellow-heads were busy feeding their young, many of which had already left the nest. From the shore, I could see dozens of them clinging to the reeds, several of which they would grasp with the claws of each foot, their little legs straddled far apart, the flexile rushes spreading out beneath their weight. There the youngsters perched, without seeming to feel any discomfort from their strained position. And what a racket they made when the parent birds returned from an excursion to distant meadows and lawns, with bill-some tidbits! They were certainly a hungry lot of bairns. When I waded out into the shallow water toward their rushy home, the old birds became quite uneasy, circling about above me like the red-wings, and uttering a harsh blackbird "chack," varied at intervals by a loud, and not unmusical, chirp.

You should see the nest of the yellow-head. It is really a fine structure, showing no small amount of artistic skill--a plaited cup, looking almost as if it had been woven by human hands, the rushes of the rim and sides folding the supporting reeds in their loops. Thus the nest and its reedy pillars are firmly bound together. I waded out to a clump of rushes and found one nest with three eggs in its softly felted cup--the promise, no doubt, of a belated, or possibly a second, brood.

This mountain lake was also the abode of a number of species of ducks, not all of which could be identified, on account of the distance they constantly put between themselves and the observer. Flocks of them floated like light, feathered craft upon the silvery bosom of the lake, now pursuing one another, now drifting lazily, now diving, and anon playing many attractive gambols.

One of the most curious ducks I have ever seen was the ruddy duck, called in the scientific manuals Erismatura rubida. As I sat on a rock on the shore, watching the aquatic fowl, one of the male ruddy ducks, accompanied by three or four females, swam out from the reeds into an open space where I could see him plainly with my field-glass. A beautiful picture he presented, as he glided proudly about on the water, surrounded by his devoted harem. Imagine, if you can, how regal he must have appeared--his broad, flat bill, light blue, widening out at the commissure, and seeming to shade off into the large white cheeks, which looked like snowy puffballs on the sides of his head; his crown, black and tapering; his neck, back, and sides, a rich, glossy brownish-red; his lower parts, "silky, silvery white, 'watered' with dusky, yielding, gray undulations"; and his wing-coverts and jauntily perked-up tail, black. If that was not a picture worthy of an artist's brush I have never seen one in the outdoor world.

No less quaint was his conduct. That he was proud and self-conscious, no one seeing him could doubt; and it was just as plain from his consequential mien, that he was posing before his train of plainly clad wives, who, no doubt, looked upon him as the greatest "catch" of the lake. Unlike most ducks, in swimming this haughty major carries his head erect, and even bent backward at a sharp angle; and his short tail is cocked up and bent forward, so that his glossy back forms a graceful half-circle or more, and does not slope downward, as do the backs of most ducks on the water.

Of all the odd gestures, this fellow's carried off the palm. He would draw his head up and back, then thrust it forward a few inches, extend his blue bill in a horizontal line, and at the same time emit a low, coarse squawk that I could barely hear. Oddly enough, all the females, staid as they were, imitated their liege lord's deportment. It was their way of protesting against my ill-bred intrusion into their demesne.

Presently a second male came out into the open space, accompanied by a retinue of wives, and then a third emerged, similarly attended. With this there was a challenging among the rivals that was interesting to witness; they fairly strutted about on the water, now advancing, now retreating, and occasionally almost, but never quite, closing in combat. Sometimes one would pursue another for a rod or more, in a swift rush that would make the spray fly and cut a swath on the smooth bosom of the lake.

Several coots now appeared on the scene. Between them and the ruddy ducks there seemed to be a feud of more or less intensity, each being on the offensive or the defensive as the exigencies of naval warfare demanded. Once I was moved to laughter as a coot made a fierce dash toward one of the ducks, and was almost upon her, and I thought she was destined to receive a severe trouncing, when she suddenly dodged her pursuer by diving. He just as suddenly gave up the chase, looking as if it were a case of "sour grapes," anyway.

After watching the antics of these birds for a long time, I turned my attention to another pretty scene,--a pair of coots leading their family of eight or ten little ones out into the clear area from their hiding-place among the reeds, presenting a picture of unruffled domestic bliss. How sweet and innocent the little coots were! Instead of the black heads and necks of their parents, and the white bills and frontal bones, these parts were tinted with red, which appeared quite bright and gauze-like in the sunshine.

The process of feeding the juvenile birds was interesting. The parents would swim about, then suddenly dip their heads into the water, or else dive clear under, coming up with slugs in their bills. Turning to the youngsters, which were always close upon their heels--or perhaps I would better say their tails--they would hold out their bills, when the little ones would swim up and pick off the toothsome morsel. It must not be supposed that the bantlings opened their mouths, as most young birds do, to receive the tidbits. No, indeed! That is not coot vogue. The little ones picked the insects from the sides of the papa's or mamma's beak, turning their own little heads cunningly to one side as they helped themselves to their luncheon.

The other waterfowl of the lake acted in an ordinary way, and therefore need no description. It was strange, however, that this was the only lake seen in all my Rocky Mountain touring where I found waterfowl. At Seven Lakes, Moraine Lake, and others in the vicinity of Pike's Peak, not a duck, crane, or coot was to be seen; and the same was true of Cottonwood Lake, twelve miles from Buena Vista, right in the heart of the rugged mountains.

Two facts may account for the abundance of birds at the little lake near Buena Vista; first, here they were protected from gunners and pot hunters by the owner, whose residence commanded a full view of the whole area; and, second, large spaces of the upper end of the lake was thickly grown with flags and rushes, which were cut off from the shore by a watery space of considerable breadth. In this place these birds found coverts from enemies and suitable sites for their nests.

A BIRD MISCELLANY

It shall be my purpose in this chapter to describe with more or less fulness a number of Rocky Mountain birds which have either not been mentioned in previous chapters or have received only casual attention.

On reaching Colorado one is surprised to find none of our common blue jays which are so abundant in the Eastern and Middle States. In my numerous Rocky Mountain jaunts not one was seen. Yet this region does not need to go begging for jays, only they belong to different groups of the Garrulin?subfamily. The most abundant and conspicuous of these western forms are the long-crested jays, so called on account of the long tuft of black feathers adorning the occiput. This distinguishing mark is not like the firm pyramidal crest of the eastern jay, but is longer and narrower, and so flexible that it sways back and forth as the bird flits from branch to branch or takes a hop-skip-and-jump over the ground. Its owner can raise and lower it at will.

The forehead of this jay is prettily sprinkled with white; his head and neck are black, in decided contrast with the umber-brown of the back; his rump and belly are pale blue, and his wings and tail are rich indigo-blue, somewhat iridescent and widely barred with black. Thus it will be seen that he has quite a different costume from that of our eastern jay, with his gaudy trimmings of white and black and purplish blue. The westerner cannot boast of cristata's dressy black collar, but otherwise he is more richly attired, although he may not be quite so showy.

The long-crested jays have a wide range among the mountains, breeding from the base of the foothills to the timber-line, although their nests are not commonly found below an altitude of seven thousand feet. In many places from nine to eleven thousand feet up the acclivities of the mountains they were seen flitting among the pines or the quaking asps. Like their eastern relatives, some individuals seem to prefer the society of man, dwelling in the villages or in the vicinity of country homes, while others choose the most secluded and solitary localities for their habitat. The fact is, I rarely made an excursion anywhere without sooner or later discovering that these jays had pre-empted the place for feeding or breeding purposes, sometimes with loud objurgations bidding me be gone, and at other times making no to-do whatever over my intrusion. Perhaps the proximity or remoteness of their nests was the chief cause of this variableness in their behavior.

A pretty picture is one of these jays mounting from branch to branch around the stem of a pine tree, from the lower limbs to the top, as if he were ascending a spiral staircase. This seems to be one of their regulation habits when they find themselves under inspection. If you intrude on their domestic precincts, their cry is quite harsh, and bears no resemblance to the quaint calls of the eastern jays; nor does the plaintive note of the eastern representative, so frequently heard in the autumnal woods, ever issue from any of the numerous jay throats of the West.

Far be it from me to blacken the reputation of any bird, but there is at least circumstantial evidence that the long-crested jay, like his eastern cousin, is a nest robber; for such birds as robins, tanagers, flycatchers, and vireos make war upon him whenever he comes within their breeding districts, and this would indicate that they are only too well aware of his predatory habits. More than that, he has the sly and stealthy manners of the sneak-thief and the brigand. Of course, he is by no means an unmixed evil, for you will often see him leaping about on the lawns, capturing beetles and worms which would surely be injurious to vegetation if allowed to live and multiply.

There are other jays in the Rockies that deserve attention. The Rocky Mountain jay--Perisoneus canadensis capitalis--is a bird of the higher altitudes, remaining near the timber-line all the year round, braving the most rigorous weather and the fiercest mountain storms during the winter. Although not an attractive species, his hardiness invests him with not a little interest. One can imagine him seeking a covert in the dense pineries when a storm sweeps down from the bald, snow-mantled summits, squawking his disapproval of the ferocity of old Boreas, and yet able to resist his most violent onsets.

Early in April, at an altitude of from eight thousand to eleven thousand five hundred feet, these jays begin to breed. At that height this is long before the snow ceases to fall; indeed, on the twentieth of June, while making the descent from Pike's Peak, I was caught in a snowfall that gave the ground quite a frosty aspect for a few minutes. One can readily fancy, therefore, that the nests of these birds are often surrounded with snow, and that the bantlings may get their first view of the world in the swirl of a snow-squall. The nests are built in pine bushes and trees at various distances from the ground. Of all the hurly-burlies ever heard, that which these birds are able to make when you go near their nests, or discover them, bears off the palm, their voices being as raucous as a buzz-saw, fairly setting your teeth on edge.

Those of us who live in the East are so accustomed to the adjective "blue" in connection with the jay that we are surprised to find that P. c. capitalis wears no blue whatever, but dons a sombre suit of leaden gray, somewhat relieved by the blackish shade of the wings and tail, with their silvery or frosted lustre. He is certainly not an attractive bird, either in dress or in form, for he appears very "thick-headed" and lumpish, as if he scarcely knew enough to seek shelter in a time of storm; but, of course, a bird that contrives to coax a livelihood out of such unpromising surroundings must possess a fine degree of intelligence, and, therefore, cannot be so much of a dullard as his appearance would indicate.

He has some interesting ways, too, as will be seen from the following quotation from a Colorado writer: "White-headed, grave, and sedate, he seems a very paragon of propriety, and if you appear to be a suitable personage, he will be apt to give you a bit of advice. Becoming confidential, he sputters out a lot of nonsense which causes you to think him a veritable 'whiskey Jack.' Yet, whenever he is disposed, a more bland, mind-your-own-business appearing bird will be hard to find; as will also many small articles around camp after one of his visits, for his whimsical brain has a great fancy for anything which may be valuable to you, but perfectly useless to himself." This habit of purloining has won him the title of "camp robber" among the people of the Rocky Mountains.

Woodhouse's jay, also peculiar to the Rocky Mountain region, is mostly to be found along the base of the foothills and the lower wooded mountains. While he may be called a "blue" jay, having more of that color in his plumage than even the long-crested, he belongs to the Aphelcoma group--that is, he is without a crest.

Every observer of eastern feathered folk is familiar with our "little boy blue," the indigo-bird, whose song is such a rollicking and saucy air, making you feel as if the little lyrist were chaffing you. In Colorado, however, you do not meet this animated chunk of blue, but another little bird that belongs to the same group, called the "painted finches," although their plumes are not painted any more than those of other species. This bird is the lazuli bunting. He wears a great deal of blue, but it is azure, and not indigo, covering the head, neck, most of the upper parts, and the lining of the wings; and, as if to give variety to the bird's attire, the nape and back are prettily shaded with brown, and the wings and tail with black. But his plumage is still more variegated, for he bears a conspicuous white spot on the greater wing-coverts, and his breast is daintily tinted with chestnut-brown, abruptly cut off from the blue of the throat, while the remaining under parts are snowy white. From this description it will be seen that he is quite unlike the indigo-bird, which has no brown or white in his cerulean attire. Handsome as Master Indigo is, the lazuli finch, with his sextet of hues, is a more showily dressed bird; in fact, a lyric in colors.

The habits of the two birds are quite similar. However, the lazuli seemed to be much shyer than his relative, for the latter is a familiar figure at the border of our eastern woodlands, about our country homes, and even in the neighborhood of our town dwellings, when there are bushes and trees close at hand. My saunterings among the mountains took me into the haunts of the lazulis, but I regret to have to confess that all my alertness was of so little avail that I saw only three males and one female. One day, while rambling among the cottonwoods that broidered the creek flowing south of Colorado Springs, I was brought to a standstill by a sharp chirp, and the next moment a pair of lazulis appeared on the lower branches and twigs of a tree. There they sat quiet enough, watching me keenly, but allowing me to peer at them at will with my field-glass. I could not understand why birds that otherwise were so shy should now permit a prolonged inspection and manifest so little anxiety; but perhaps they reasoned that they had been discovered anyway, and there was no need of pretending that no lazulis dwelt in the neighborhood. How elegant the little husband looked in his variegated attire! The wife was soberly clad in warm brown, slightly streaked with dusk, but she was trig and pretty and worthy of her more richly apparelled spouse. In the bushes below I found a well-made nest, which I felt morally certain belonged to the little couple that was keeping such faithful surveillance over it. As yet it contained no eggs.

In order to make certainty doubly sure, I visited the place a week or so later, and found that my previous conclusion had been correct. I flushed the little madame from the nest, and saw her flit with a chirp to the twigs above, where she sat quietly watching her visitor, exhibiting no uneasiness whatever about her cot in the bushes with its three precious eggs. It was pleasing to note the calmness and dignity with which she regarded me. But where was that important personage, the little husband? He was nowhere to be seen, although I lingered about the charmed spot for over two hours, hoping to get at least a glimpse of him. A friend, who understands the sly ways of the lazulis, suggested that very likely the male was watching me narrowly all the while from a safe hiding-place in the dense foliage of some tree not far away.

My friend told me that I would not be able to distinguish the song of the lazuli from those of the summer and mountain warblers. We shall see whether he was right. One evening I was searching for a couple of blue grosbeaks at the border of Colorado Springs, where I had previously seen them, when a loud, somewhat percussive song, much like the summer warbler's, burst on my ear, coming from a clump of willow bushes hard by the stream. At once I said to myself, "That is not the summer warbler's trill. It resembles the challenging song of the indigo-bird, only it is not quite so loud and defiant. A lazuli finch's song, or I am sadly astray! Let me settle the question now."

I did settle it to my great satisfaction, for, after no little effort, I succeeded in obtaining a plain view of the elusive little lyrist, and, sure enough, it proved to be the lazuli finch. Metaphorically I patted myself with a great deal of self-complacency, as I muttered: "The idea of Mr. Aiken's thinking I had so little discrimination! I know that hereafter I shall be able to detect the lazuli's peculiar intonations every time." So I walked home in a very self-confident frame of mind. A few days later I heard another song lilting down from the upper branches of a small tree. "Surely that is the lazuli again," I muttered. "I know that voice." For a while I eyed the tree, and presently caught sight of the little triller, and behold, it was--a summer warbler! All my self-complacency vanished in a moment; I wasn't cock-sure of anything; and I am obliged to confess that I was led astray in a similar manner more than once afterward. It may indicate an odd psychological condition to make the claim;

but, absurd or not, I am disposed to believe that, whenever I really heard the lazuli, I was able to recognize his song with a fair degree of certainty, but when I heard the summer warbler I was thrown into more or less confusion, not being quite sure whether it was that bird or the other.

The most satisfactory lazuli song I heard was on the western side of the range, at the resort called Glenwood. This time, as was usually the case, I heard the little triller before seeing him, and was sure it was Passerina amoena, as the bunting strains were plainly discernible. He was sitting on a telephone wire, and did not flit away as I stood below and peered at him through my glass, and admired his trig and handsome form. I studied his song, and tried to fix the peculiar intonations in my mind, and felt positive that I could never be caught again--but I was.[8]

[8] In the foregoing remarks the lazuli finches have been represented as excessively shy. So they were in 1899 in the neighborhoods then visited. Strangely enough, in the vicinity of Denver in 1901, these birds were abundant and as easily approached and studied as are the indigoes of the East. See the chapter entitled, "Plains and Foothills."

The lazuli finch does not venture very high into the mountains, seldom reaching an altitude of more than seven thousand feet. He is a lover of the plains, the foothills, and the lower ranges of the mountains. In this respect he differs from some other little birds, which seek a summer home in the higher regions. On the southern slope of Pike's Peak, a little below the timber-line, I found a dainty little bird which was a stranger to me. It was Audubon's warbler. At first sight I decided that he must be the myrtle warbler, but was compelled to change my conclusion when I got a glimpse of his throat, which was golden yellow, whereas the throat of Dendroica coronata is pure white. Then, too, the myrtle warbler is only a migrant in Colorado, passing farther north to breed. Audubon's, it must be said, has extremely rich habiliments, his upper parts being bluish-ash, streaked with black, his belly and under tail-coverts white, and his breast in high feather, black, prettily skirted with gray or invaded with white from below; but his yellow spots, set like gleaming gold in various parts of his plumage, constitute his most marked embellishment, being found on the crown, rump, throat, and each side of the chest.

On my first excursion to some meadows and wooded low-grounds south of Colorado Springs, while listening to a concert given by western meadow-larks, my attention was attracted to a large, black bird circling about the fields and then alighting on a fence-post. My first thought was: "It is only a crow blackbird." But on second thought I decided that the crow blackbird did not soar and circle about in this manner. At all events, there seemed to be something slightly peculiar about this bird's behavior, so I went nearer to inspect him, when he left his perch on the post, flapped around over the meadow, and finally flew to a large, partially decayed cottonwood tree in a pasture field. If I could believe my eyes, he clung to the upright stems of the branches after the style of a woodpecker! That was queer indeed--a woodpecker that looked precisely like a blackbird! Such a featherland oddity was certainly foreign to any of my calculations; for, it must be remembered, this was prior to my making acquaintance with Williamson's sapsucker.

Closer inspection proved that this bird was actually hitching up and down the branches of the tree in the regular woodpecker fashion. Presently he slipped into a hole in a large limb, and the loud, eager chirping of young birds was heard. It was not long before his mate appeared, entered the cavity, and fed the clamorous brood. The birds proved to be Lewis's woodpeckers, another distinctly western type. My field-glass soon clearly brought out their peculiar markings.

A beautiful bird-skin, bought of Mr. Charles E. Aiken, now lies on my desk and enables me to describe the fine habiliments of this kind from an actual specimen. His upper parts are glossy black, the sheen on the back being greenish, and that on the wings and tail bluish or purplish, according to the angle of the sun's light; a white collar prettily encircles the neck, becoming quite narrow on the nape, but widening out on the side so as to cover the entire breast and throat. This pectoral shield is mottled with black and lightly stained with buff in spots; the forehead, chin, superciliary line, and a broad space on the cheek are dyed a deep crimson; and, not least by any means, the abdomen is washed with pink, which is delicately stencilled with white, gray, and buff. A most gorgeous bird, fairly rivalling, but not distancing, Williamson's sapsucker.

By accident I made a little discovery relative to the claws of this woodpecker which, I suppose, would be true of all the Picid?family. The claws of the two fore toes are sharply curved and extremely acute, making genuine hooks, so that when I attempt to pass my finger over them the points catch at the skin. Could a better hook be contrived for enabling the bird to clamber up the trunks and branches of trees? But note: the claws of the two hind toes are not so sharply decurved, nor so acute at the points, the finger slipping readily over them. Who can deny the evidence of design in nature? The fore claws are highly specialized for clinging, the very purpose for which they are needed, while the hind claws, being used for a different purpose--only that of support--are moulded over a different pattern.

Like our common red-head, this bird has the habit of soaring out into the air and nabbing insects on the wing. The only other pair of these woodpeckers I was so fortunate as to meet with were found in the ravine leading up from Buena Vista to Cottonwood Lake.[9] Their nest was in a dead tree by the roadside. While the first couple had been entirely silent, one of the second pair chirped somewhat uneasily when I lingered beneath his tree, suspecting, no doubt, that I had sinister designs upon his nest. Unlike some of their kinsmen, these pickers of wood seem to be quiet and dignified, not given to much demonstration, and are quite leisurely in their movements both on the branch and on the wing.

[9] Two years later a pair were seen on a mountain near Golden, Colorado, and probably twenty individuals were watched a long time from a canyon above Boulder as they circled gracefully over the mountains, catching insects on the wing.

One day, when walking up Ute Pass, celebrated both for its magnificent scenery and its Indian history, I first saw the water-ousel. I had been inspecting Rainbow Falls, and was duly impressed with its attractiveness. Thinking I had lingered long enough, I turned away and clambered up the rocky wall below the falls towards the road above. As I did so, a loud, bell-like song rang above the roar of the water. On looking down into the ravine, I saw a mouse-colored bird, a little smaller than the robin, his tail perked up almost vertically, scuttling about on the rocks below and dipping his body in an expressive way like the "tip-up" sandpiper. Having read about this bird, I at once recognized it as the water-ousel. My interest in everything else vanished. This was one of the birds I had made my pilgrimage to the Rockies to study. It required only a few minutes to scramble down into the ravine again.

Breathlessly I watched the little bird. Its queer teetering is like that of some of the wrens, accentors, and water-thrushes. Now it ran to the top of a rock and stood dipping and eying me narrowly, flirting its bobby tail; now it flew to one of the steep, almost vertical walls of rock and scrambled up to a protuberance; then down again to the water; then, to my intense delight, it plunged into the limpid stream, and came up the next moment with a slug or water-beetle in its bill. Presently it flew over to the opposite wall, its feet slipping on the wet rocks, and darted into a small crevice just below the foot of the falls, gave a quick poke with its beak and flitted away--minus the tidbit it had held in its bill.

RAINBOW FALLS

When the sun strikes the spray and mist at the proper angle, a beautiful rainbow is painted on the face of the falls. At the time of the author's visit to this idyllic spot a pair of water-ousels had chosen it for a summer residence. They flew from the rocks below to the top of the falls, hugging close to the rushing torrent. In returning, they darted in one swift plunge from the top to the bottom, alighting on the rocks below. With the utmost abandon they dived into the seething waters at the foot of the falls, usually emerging with a slug or beetle in their bills for the nestlings. Shod with tall rubber boots, the writer waded close up to the foot of the falls in search of the dipper's nest, which was set in a cleft of the rocks a few inches above the water, in the little shadowed cavern at the left of the stream. The pointed rock wrapped in mist, almost in the line of the plunging tide, was a favorite perch for the dippers.

Ah! my propitious stars shone on me that day with special favor. I had found not only the water-ousel itself, but also its nest. Suddenly water-ousel number two, the mate of number one, appeared on the scene, dipped, scanned me closely, flew to the slippery wall, darted to the cranny, and deposited its morsel, as its spouse had done. This time I heard the chirping of the youngsters. Before examining the nest I decided to watch the performances of the parent birds, which soon cast off all the restraint caused for a moment by my presence, taking me, no doubt, for the ordinary sightseer who overlooks them altogether.

Again and again the birds plunged into the churning flood at the foot of the falls, sometimes remaining under water what seemed a long while, and always coming to the surface with a delicacy for the nestlings. They were able to dip into the swift, white currents and wrestle with them without being washed away. Of course, the water would sometimes carry them down stream, but never more than a few inches, and never to a point where they could be injured. They were perfect masters of the situation. They simply slipped in and out like living chunks of cork. Their coats were waterproof, all they needed to do being to shake off the crystal drops now and then.

Their flight up the almost perpendicular face of the falls was one of graceful celerity. Up, up, they would mount only a few inches from the dashing current, and disappear upstream in search of food. In returning, they would sweep down over the precipitous falls with the swiftness of arrows, stopping themselves lightly with their outspread wings before reaching the rocks below. From a human point of view it was a frightful plunge; from the ousel point of view it was an every-day affair.

After watching the tussle between ousel and water for a long time, I decided to take a peep at their nursery. In order to do this I was compelled to wade into the stream a little below the falls, through mist and spray; yet such humid quarters were the natural habitat and playground of these interesting cinclids. And there the nest was, set in a cleft about a foot and a half above the water, its outer walls kept moist by the spray which constantly dashed against them from the falls. The water was also dripping from the rock that over-hung the nest and formed its roof. A damp, uncanny place for a bird's domicile, you would naturally suppose, but the little lovers of cascades knew what they were about. Only the exterior of the thick, moss-covered walls were moist. Within, the nest was dry and cosey. It was an oval structure, set in its rocky cleft like a small oven, with an opening at the front. And there in the doorway cuddled the two fledglings, looking out at the dripping walls and the watery tumult, but kept warm and comfortable. I could not resist touching them and caressing their little heads, considering it quite an ornithological triumph for one day to find a pair of water-ousels, discover a nest, and place my finger upon the crowns of the nestlings.

Scores of tourists visited the famous falls every day, some of them lingering long in the beautiful place, and yet the little ousels had gone on with their nest-building and brood-rearing, undisturbed by human spectators. I wondered whether many of the visitors noticed the birds, and whether any one but myself had discovered their nest. Indeed, their little ones were safe enough from human meddling, for one could not see the nest without wading up the stream into the sphere of the flying mists.

The natural home of Cinclus mexicanus is the Rocky Mountains, to which he is restricted, not being known anywhere else on this continent. He is the only member of the dipper family in North America. There is one species in South America, and another in Europe. He loves the mountain stream, with its dashing rapids and cascades. Indeed, he will erect his oven-like cottage nowhere else, and it must be a fall and not a mere ripple or rapid. Then from this point as a centre--or, rather, the middle point of a wavering line--he forages up and down the babbling, meandering brook, feeding chiefly, if not wholly, on water insects. Strange to say, he never leaves the streams, never makes excursions to the country roundabout, never flies over a mountain ridge or divide to reach another valley, but simply pursues the winding streams with a fidelity that deserves praise for its very singleness of purpose. No "landlubber" he. It is said by one writer that the dipper has never been known to alight on a tree, preferring a rock or a piece of driftwood beside the babbling stream; yet he has the digits and claws of the passeres, among which he is placed systematically. He is indeed an anomaly, though a very engaging one. Should he wish to go to another canyon, he will simply follow the devious stream he is on to its junction with the stream of the other valley; then up the second defile. His flight is exceedingly swift. His song is a loud, clear, cheerful strain, the very quintessence of gladness as it mingles with the roar of the cataracts.

Farther up Ute Pass I found another nest, which was placed right back of a cascade, so that the birds had to dash through a curtain of spray to reach their cot. They also were feeding their young, and I could see them standing on a rock beneath the shelf, tilting their bodies and scanning me narrowly before diving into the cleft where the nest was hidden. This nest, being placed back of the falls, could not be reached.

In Bear Creek canyon I discovered another inaccessible nest, which was placed in a fissure at the very foot of the falls and only an inch or two above the agitated waters. There must have been a cavity running back into the rock, else the nest would have been kept in a soggy condition all the time.

Perhaps the most interesting dipper's nest I found was one at the celebrated Seven Falls in the south Cheyenne Canyon. On the face of the cliff by the side of the lowest fall there was a cleft, in which the nest was placed, looking like a large bunch of moss and grass. My glass brought the structure so near that I could plainly see three little heads protruding from the doorway. There were a dozen or more people about the falls at the time, who made no attempt at being quiet, and yet the parent birds flew fearlessly up to the nest with tidbits in their bills, and were greeted with loud, impatient cries from three hungry mouths, which were opened wide to receive the food. The total plunge of the stream over the Seven Falls is hundreds of feet, and yet the adult birds would toss themselves over the abyss with reckless abandon, stop themselves without apparent effort in front of their cleft, and thrust the gathered morsels into the little yellow-lined mouths. It was an aerial feat that made our heads dizzy. This pair of birds did not fly up the face of the falls in ascending to the top, as did those at Rainbow Falls, but clambered up the wall of the cliff close to the side of the roaring cataract, aiding themselves with both claws and wings. When gathering food below the falls, they would usually, in going or returning, fly in a graceful curve over the heads of their human visitors.

Although the dipper is not a web-footed bird, and is not classed by the naturalists among the aquatic fowl, but is, indeed, a genuine passerine, yet he can swim quite dexterously on the surface of the water. However, his greatest strength and skill are shown in swimming under water, where he propels himself with his wings, often to a considerable distance, either with or against the current. Sometimes he will allow the current to carry him a short distance down the stream, but he is always able to stop himself at a chosen point. "Ever and anon," says Mr. John Muir, in his attractive book on "The Mountains of California," "while searching for food in the rushing stream, he sidles out to where the too powerful current carries him off his feet; then he dexterously rises on the wing and goes gleaning again in shallower places." So it seems that our little acrobat is equal to every emergency that may arise in his adventurous life.

In winter, when the rushing mountain streams are flowing with the sludge of the half-melted snow, so that he cannot see the bottom, where most of his delicacies lie, he betakes himself to the quieter stretches of the rivers, or to the mill ponds or mountain lakes, where he finds clearer and smoother water, although a little deeper than he usually selects. Such weather does not find him at the end of his resources; no, indeed! Having betaken himself to a lake, he does not at once plunge into its depths after the manner of a duck, but finding a perch on a snag or a fallen pine, he sits there a moment, and then, flying out thirty or forty yards, "he alights with a dainty glint on the surface, swims about, looks down, finally makes up his mind, and disappears with a sharp stroke of his wings." So says Mr. John Muir, who continues: "After feeding for two or three minutes he suddenly reappears, showers the water from his wings with one vigorous shake, and rises abruptly into the air as if pushed up from beneath, comes back to his perch, sings a few minutes, and goes out to dive again; thus coming and going, singing and diving, at the same place for hours."

The depths to which the cinclid dives for the food on the bottom is often from fifteen to twenty feet. When he selects a river instead of a lake for his winter bathing, its waters, like those of the shallower streams, may also contain a large quantity of sludge, thus rendering them opaque even to the sharp little eyes of the dipper. Then what does he do? He has a very natural and cunning way of solving this problem; he simply seeks a deep portion of the river and dives through the turbid water to the clear water beneath, where he can plainly see the "goodies" on the bottom.

It must not be thought that this little bird is mute amid all the watery tumult of his mountain home, for he is a rare vocalist, his song mingling with the ripple and gurgle and roar of the streams that he haunts. Nor does he sing only in the springtime, but all the year round, on stormy days as well as fair. During Indian summer, when the streams are small, and silence broods over many a mountain solitude, the song of the ousel falls to its lowest ebb; but when winter comes and the streams are converted into rolling torrents, he resumes his vocal efforts, which reach their height in early summer. Thus it would seem that the bird's mood is the gayest when his favorite stream is dashing at its noisiest and most rapid pace down the steep mountain defiles. The clamor of the stream often drowns the song of the bird, the movement of his mandibles being seen when not a sound from his music-box can be heard. There must be a feeling of fellowship between the bird and the stream he loves so well.

You will not be surprised to learn that the dipper is an extremely hardy bird. No snowstorm, however violent, can discourage him, but in the midst of it all he sings his most cheerful lays, as if defying all the gods of the winds. While other birds, even the hardy nuthatches, often succumb to discouragement in cold weather, and move about with fluffed-up feathers, the very picture of dejection-- not so the little dipper, who always preserves his cheerful temper, and is ready to say, in acts, if not in words: "Isn't this the jolliest weather you ever saw?" Away up in Alaska, where the glaciers hold perpetual sway, this bird has been seen in the month of November as glad and blithesome as were his comrades in the summery gorges of New Mexico.

PLAINS AND FOOTHILLS

The foregoing chapters contain a recital of observations made in the neighborhood of Colorado Springs and in trips on the plains and among the mountains in that latitude. Two years later--that is, in 1901--the rambler's good angel again smiled upon him and made possible another tour among the Colorado mountains. This time he made Denver, instead of Colorado Springs, the centre of operations; nor did he go alone, his companion being an active boy of fourteen who has a penchant for Butterflies, while that of the writer, as need scarcely be said, is for the Birds--in our estimation, the two cardinal B's of the English language. Imagine two inveterate ramblers, then, with two such enchanting hobbies, set loose on the Colorado plains and in the mountains, with the prospect of a month of uninterrupted indulgence in their manias!

In the account of my first visit, most of the species met with were described in detail both as to their habits and personal appearance. In the present record no such thing will be necessary so far as the same species were observed, and therefore the chief objects of the following chapters will be, first, to note the diversities in the avian fauna of the two regions; second, to give special attention to such birds as either were not seen in my first visit or were for some cause partly overlooked; and, third, to trace the peculiar transitions in bird life in passing from the plains about Denver to the crest of Gray's Peak, including jaunts to several other localities.

In my rambles in the neighborhood of Denver only a few species not previously described were observed, and yet there were some noteworthy points of difference in the avi-fauna of the two latitudes, which are only about seventy-five miles apart. It will perhaps be remembered that, in the vicinity of Colorado Springs and Manitou, the pretty lazuli buntings were quite rare and exceedingly shy, only two or three individuals having been seen. The reverse was the case in the suburbs of Denver and on the irrigated plains between that city and the mountains, and also in the neighborhood of Boulder, where in all suitable haunts the lazulis were constantly at my elbow, lavish enough of their pert little melodies to satisfy the most exacting, and almost as familiar and approachable as the indigo-birds of the East. It is possible that, for the most part, the blue-coated beauties prefer a more northern latitude than Colorado Springs for the breeding season.

At the latter place I failed to find the burrowing owl, although there can be little doubt of his presence there, especially out on the plains. Not far from Denver one of these uncanny, sepulchral birds was seen, having been frightened from her tunnel as I came stalking near it. She flew over the brow of the hill in her smooth, silent way, and uttered no syllable of protest as I examined her domicile--or, rather, the outside of it. Scattered about the dark doorway were a number of bones, feathers, and the skin of a frog, telling the story of the table set by this underground dweller before her nestlings. She might have put up the crossbones and skull as a sign at the entrance to her burrow, or even placed there the well-known Dantean legend, "All hope abandon, ye who enter here," neither of which would have been more suggestive than the telltale litter piled up before her door. When I chased her from her hiding-place, she flew down the hill and alighted on a fence-post in the neighborhood of her nest, uttering several screechy notes as I came near her again, as if she meant to say that I was carrying the joke a little too far in pursuing her about. Presently she circled away on oily wings, and I saw her no more.

So little enthusiasm does such a bird stir within me that I felt too lazy to follow her about on the arid plain. It may be interesting as a matter of scientific information to know that the burrowing owl breeds in a hole in the ground, and keeps company with the prairie dog and the rattlesnake, but a bird that lives in a gloomy, malodorous cave, whose manners are far from attractive, and whose voice sounds as strident as a buzz-saw--surely such a bird can cast no spell upon the observer who is interested in the authentic side of bird nature. A recent writer, in describing "A Buzzards' Banquet," asks a couple of pregnant questions: "Is there anything ugly out of doors? Can the ardent, sympathetic lover of nature ever find her unlovely?" To the present writer these questions present no Chinese puzzle. He simply brushes all speculation and theorizing aside by responding "Yes," to both interrogatories, on the principle that it is sometimes just as well to cut the Gordian knot as to waste precious time trying to untie it. The burrowing owl makes me think of a denizen of the other side of the river Styx, and why should one try to love that which nature has made unattractive, especially when one cannot help one's feeling?

In the preceding chronicles no mention, I believe, has been made of one little bird that deserves more than a mere obiter dictum. My first meeting with the blithesome house-finch of the West occurred in the city of Denver, in 1899. It could not properly be called a formal presentment, but was none the less welcome on that account. I had scarcely stepped out upon the busy street before my ear was accosted by a kind of half twitter and half song that was new to me. "Surely that is not the racket of the English sparrow; it is too musical," I remarked to a friend walking by my side.

Peering among the trees and houses, I presently focussed my field-glass upon a small, finch-like bird whose coat was striped with gray and brown, and whose face, crown, breast, and rump were beautifully tinged or washed with crimson, giving him quite a dressy appearance. What could this chipper little city chap be, with his trig form and well-bred manners, in such marked contrast with those of the swaggering English sparrow? Afterwards he was identified as the house-finch, which rejoices in the high-sounding Latin name of Carpodacus mexicanus frontalis. His distribution is restricted to the Rocky Mountain district chiefly south of the fortieth parallel of north latitude.

He is certainly an attractive species, and I wish we could offer sufficient inducements to bring him east. A bird like him is a boon and an ornament to the streets and parks of any city that he graces with his presence and enlivens with his songs. No selfish recluse is he; no, indeed! In no dark gulch or wilderness, far from human neighborhood, does he sulkily take up his abode, but prefers the companionship of man to the solitudes of nature, declaring in all his conduct that he likes to be where there are "folks." In this respect he bears likeness to the English sparrow; but let it be remembered that there the analogy stops. Even his chirruping is musical as he flies overhead, or makes his caveat from a tree or a telegraph wire against your ill-bred espionage. He and his plainly clad little spouse build a neat cottage for their bairns about the houses, but do not clog the spouting and make themselves a nuisance otherwise, as is the habit of their English cousins.

This finch is a minstrel, not of the first class, still one that merits a high place among the minor songsters; and, withal, he is generous with his music. You might call him a kind of urban Arion, for there is real melody in his little score. As he is an early riser, his matin voluntaries often mingled with my half-waking dreams in the morning at dawn's peeping, and I loved to hear it too well to be angry for being aroused at an unseasonable hour. The song is quite a complicated performance at its best, considerably prolonged and varied, running up and down the chromatic scale with a swing and gallop, and delivered with great rapidity, as if the lyrist were in a hurry to have done, so that he could get at something else.

In my rambles he was found not only in the cities of the plains (Denver, Colorado Springs, and Pueblo), but also in many of the mountain towns and villages visited, Leadville, over ten thousand feet skyward, being, I believe, one of the exceptions, while Silver Plume and Graymont were others. He does not fancy altitudes, I take it, much over eight thousand feet. In the villages of Red Cliff and Glenwood, both beyond the continental divide, he was the same sprightly citizen, making himself very much at home.

Much as this finch cherishes the society of man, he is quite wary and suspicious, and does not fancy being watched. As long as you go on your way without seeming to notice him, he also goes his way, coming into plain sight and chirping and singing; but just stop to watch him with your binocular, and see how quickly he will take alarm, dart away, and ensconce himself behind a clump of foliage, uttering a protest which seems to say, "Why doesn't that old fellow go about his own business?" If in some way the American house-finch could be persuaded to come east, and the English sparrow could be given papers of extradition, the exchange would be a relief and a benefit to the whole country.

Some idyllic days were spent in sauntering about Golden, which keeps guard at the entrance of Clear Creek Canyon, and has tucked itself in a beautiful valley among the foothills, which in turn stand sentinel over it. In the village itself and along the bush-fringed border of the creek below, as well as in the little park at its border, there were many birds, nearly all of which have been described in the previous chapters. However, several exceptions are worthy of note. A matted copse a mile and a half below the town afforded a hiding-place for three young or female redstarts, which were "playing butterfly," as usual, and chanting their vivacious little tunes. These and several near Boulder were the only redstarts seen in my Colorado wanderings, although Professor Cooke says they breed sparingly on the plains, and a little more commonly in the mountains to an altitude of eight thousand feet, while one observer saw a female in July at the timber-line, which is three thousand feet above the normal range of the species. Why did not this birdlet remain within the bounds set by the scientific guild? Suit for contempt of court should be brought against it. Redstarts must have been very scarce in the regions over which I rambled, else I certainly should have noticed birds that are so fearless and so lavish of song.

One day my companion and I clambered up the steep side of a mesa some distance below Golden--that is, the base of the mesa was below the village, while its top towered far above it. A mesa was a structural portion of Colorado topography that neither of the two ramblers had yet explored, and we were anxious to know something about its resources from a natural history point of view. It was hard climbing on account of the steepness of the acclivity, its rocky character, and the thick network of bushes and brambles in many places; but "excelsior" was our motto in all our mountaineering, and we allowed no surmountable difficulties to daunt us. What birds select such steep places for a habitat? Here lived in happy domesticity the lyrical green-tailed towhee, the bird of the liquid voice, the poet laureate of the steep, bushy mountain sides, just as the water-ousel is the poet of the cascades far down in the canyons and gulches; here also thrived the spurred towhees, one of which had tucked a nest beneath a bush cradling three speckled eggs. This was the second nest of this species I had found, albeit not the last. Here also dwelt the rock wren, a little bird that was new to me and that I had not found in the latitude of Colorado Springs either east or west of the continental divide. A description of this anchorite of the rocks will be given in a later chapter. I simply pause here to remark that he has a sort of "monarch-of-all-I-survey" air as he sits on a tall sandstone rock and blows the music from his Huon's horn on the messenger breezes. His wild melodies, often sounding like a blast from a bugle, are in perfect concord with the wild and rugged acclivities which he haunts, from which he can command many a prospect that pleases, whether he glances down into the valleys or up to the silver-capped mountain peaks. One cannot help feeling--at least, after one has left his rock-strewn dwelling-place--that a kind of glamour hangs about it and him.

The loud hurly-burly of the long-tailed chat reached us from a bushy hollow not far away. So far as I could determine, this fellow is as garrulous a churl and bully as his yellow-breasted cousin so well known in the East. (Afterwards I found the chats quite numerous at Boulder.) At length we scaled the cliffs, and presently stood on the edge of the mesa, which we found to be a somewhat rolling plateau, looking much like the plains themselves in general features, with here and there a hint of verdure, on which a herd of cattle were grazing. The pasture was the buffalo grass. Does the bird-lover ask what species dwell on a treeless mesa like this? It was the home of western grassfinches, western meadow-larks, turtle doves, desert horned larks, and a little bird that was new to me, evidently Brewer's sparrow. Its favorite resort was in the low bushes growing on the border of the mesa and along the edge of the cliff. Its song was unique, the opening syllable running low on the alto clef, while the closing notes constituted a very respectable soprano. A few extremely shy sparrows flitted about in the thickets of a hollow as we began our descent, and I have no doubt they were Lincoln's sparrows.

The valley and the irrigated plain were the birds' elysium. Here we first saw and heard that captivating bird, the lark bunting, as will be fully set forth in the closing chapter. This was one of the birds that had escaped me in my first visit to Colorado, save as I had caught tantalizing glimpses of him from the car-window on the plain beyond Denver, and when I went south to Colorado Springs, I utterly failed to find him. It has been a sort of riddle to me that not one could be discovered in that vicinity, while two years later these birds were abundant on the plains both east and west of Denver. If Colorado Springs is a little too far south for them in the summer, Denver is obviously just to their liking. No less abundant were the western meadow-larks, which flew and sang with a kind of lyrical intoxication over the green alfalfa fields.

One morning we decided to walk some distance up Clear Creek Canyon. At the opening of the canyon, Brewer's blackbirds were scuttling about in the bushes that broidered the steep banks of the tumultuous stream, and a short distance up in the gorge a lazuli bunting sat on a telegraph wire and piped his merry lay. Soon the canyon narrowed, grew dark and forbidding, and the steep walls rose high on both sides, compelling the railway to creep like a half-imprisoned serpent along the foot of the cliffs; then the birds disappeared, not caring to dwell in such dark, more than half-immured places. Occasionally a magpie could be seen sailing overhead at an immense height, crossing over from one hillside to the other, turning his head as he made the transit, to get a view of the two peripatetics in the gulch below, anxious to discover whether they were bent on brigandage of any kind.

At length we reached a point where the mountain side did not look so steep as elsewhere, and we decided to scale it. From the railway it looked like a short climb, even if a little difficult, and we began it with only a slight idea of the magnitude of our undertaking. The fact is, mountain climbing is a good deal more than pastime; it amounts to work, downright hard work. In the present instance, no sooner had we gained one height than another loomed steep and challenging above us, so that we climbed the mountain by a series of immense steps or terraces. At places the acclivity was so steep that we were compelled to scramble over the rocks on all fours, and were glad to stop frequently and draw breath and rest our tired limbs. My boy comrade, having fewer things than I to lure him by the way, and being, perhaps, a little more agile as well, went far on ahead of me, often standing on a dizzy pinnacle of rock, and waving his butterfly-net or his cap in the air, and shouting at the top of his voice to encourage his lagging parent and announce his triumph as a mountaineer.

However, the birdman can never forget his hobby. There were a few birds on that precipitous mountain side, and that lent it its chief attraction. At one place a spurred towhee flitted about in a bushy clump and called much like a catbird--an almost certain proof of a nest on the steep, rocky wall far up from the roaring torrent in the gorge below. On a stony ridge still farther up, a rock wren was ringing his peculiar score, which sounds so much like a challenge, while still farther up, in a cluster of stunted pines, a long-crested jay lilted about and called petulantly, until I came near, when he swung across the canyon, and I saw him no more.

After a couple of hours of hard climbing, we reached the summit, from which we were afforded a magnificent view of the foothills, the mesas, and the stretching plains below us, while above us to the west hills rose on hills until they culminated in mighty snow-capped peaks and ridges. It must not be supposed, because the snow-mantled summits in the west loomed far above our present station, that this mountain which we had ascended was a comparatively insignificant affair. The fact is, it was of huge bulk and great height measured from its base in the canyon; almost as much of a mountain, in itself considered, as Gray's Peak. It must be borne in mind that the snowy peaks were from thirty to forty miles away, and that there is a gradual ascent the entire distance to the upper valleys and gorges which creep about the bases of the loftiest peaks and ridges. A mountain rising from the foothills may be almost as bulky and high and precipitous as one of the alpine peaks covered with eternal snow. Its actual altitude above sea-level may be less by many thousand feet, while its height from the surrounding canyons and valleys may be almost, if not quite, as great. The alpine peaks have the advantage of majesty of situation, because the general level of the country from which they rise is very high. There we stood at a sort of outdoor halfway house between the plains and the towering ridges, and I can only say that the view was superb.

There were certain kinds of birds which had brought their household gods to the mountain's crest. Lewis's woodpeckers ambled about over the summit and rocky ridges, catching insects on the wing, as is their wont. Some distance below the summit a pair of them had a nest in a dead pine snag, from the orifice of which one was seen to issue. A mother hawk was feeding a couple of youngsters on the snarly branch of a dead pine. Almost on the summit a western nighthawk sprang up from my feet. On the bare ground, without the faintest sign of a nest, lay her two speckled eggs, which she had been brooding. She swept around above the summit in immense zigzag spirals while I examined her roofless dwelling-place. It was interesting to one bird-lover, at least, to know that the nighthawk breeds in such places. Like their eastern congeners, the western nighthawks are fond of "booming." At intervals a magpie would swing across the canyon, looking from side to side, the impersonation of cautious shyness. A few rods below the crest a couple of rock wrens were flitting about some large rocks, creeping in and out among the crevices like gray mice, and at length one of them slyly fed a well-fledged youngster. This proves that these birds, like many of their congeners, are partial to a commanding lookout for a nesting site. These were the only occupants of the mountain's brow at the time of our visit, although in one of the hollows below us the spurred and green-tailed towhees were rendering a selection from Haydn's "Creation," probably "The heavens are telling."

No water was to be found from the bottom of the canyon to the summit of the mountain; all was as dry as the plain itself. The feathered tenants of the dizzy height were doubtless compelled to fly down into the gorge for drinking and bathing purposes, and then wing up again to the summit--certainly no light task for such birds as the wrens and towhees.

Before daybreak one morning I made my way to a small park on the outskirts of the village to listen to the birds' matutinal concert. The earliest singers were the western robins, which began their carols at the first hint of the coming dawn; the next to break the silence were the western wood-pewees; then the summer warblers chimed in, followed by the western grassfinches, Bullock's orioles, meadow-larks, and lark sparrows, in the order named. Before daylight had fully come a family of mountain bluebirds were taking their breakfast at the border of the park, while their human relatives were still snoring in bed. The bluebirds are governed by old-fashioned rules even in this very "modern" age, among their maxims being,--

"Early to bed and early to rise, Makes bluebirds healthy and wealthy and wise."

Just now I came across a pretty conceit of John B. Tabb, which more aptly sets off the mountain blue than it does his eastern relative, and which I cannot forbear quoting:

"When God made a host of them, One little flower lacked a stem To hold its blossom blue; So into it He breathed a song, And suddenly, with petals strong As wings, away it flew."

And there is Eben E. Rexford, who almost loses himself in a tangle of metaphors in his efforts to express his admiration of this bird with the cerulean plumes. Hark to his rhapsody:

"Winged lute that we call a bluebird, you blend in a silver strain The sound of the laughing waters, the patter of spring's sweet rain, The voice of the winds, the sunshine, and fragrance of blossoming things; Ah! you are an April poem that God has dowered with wings."

On our return to the plains from a two weeks' trip to Georgetown and Gray's Peak, we spent several days at Arvada, a village about halfway between Denver and Golden. The place was rife with birds, all of which are described in other chapters of this volume.[10] Mention need be made here only of the song-sparrows, which were seen in a bushy place through which a purling stream wound its way. Of course, they were Melospiza fasciata montana, but their clear, bell-like trills were precise copies of those of the merry lowland minstrels of the East. Special attention is called to the fact that, in my first visit to Colorado, the only place in which mountain song-sparrows were met with was Buena Vista, quite a distance up among the mountains, while in the visit now being described they were not found anywhere in the mountains, save in the vale below Cassels. They were breeding at Arvada, for a female was seen carrying a worm in her bill, and I am sure a nest might easily have been found had I not been so busily occupied in the study of other and rarer species. However, the recollection of the merry lyrists with the speckled breasts and silvery voices, brings to mind Mr. Ernest Thompson Seton's "Myth of the Song-Sparrow," from which it will be seen that this attractive bird has had something of an adventurous career:

"His mother was the Brook, his sisters were the Reeds, And they every one applauded when he sang about his deeds. His vest was white, his mantle brown, as clear as they could be, And his songs were fairly bubbling o'er with melody and glee. But an envious Neighbor splashed with mud our Brownie's coat and vest, And then a final handful threw that stuck upon his breast. The Brook-bird's mother did her best to wash the stains away, But there they stuck, and, as it seems, are very like to stay. And so he wears the splashes and the mud blotch, as you see; But his songs are bubbling over still with melody and glee."

[10] I find I have overlooked the western Maryland yellow-throat, which was seen here; also near Colorado Springs, and in several other bushy spots, only on the plains. It seldom ascends into the mountains, never far. Its song and habits are similar to those of its eastern congener.

RAMBLES ABOUT GEORGETOWN

At nine o'clock on the morning of June 22, the two ramblers boarded a Colorado and Southern train, and bowled up Clear Creek Canyon to Georgetown. Having been studying winged creatures on the plains and among the foothills, mesas, and lower mountains, we now proposed to go up among the mountains that were mountains in good earnest, and see what we could find.

The village of Georgetown nestles in a deep pocket of the mountains. The valley is quite narrow, and on three sides, save where the two branches of Clear Creek have hewn out their canyons, the ridges rise at a sharp angle to a towering height, while here and there a white-cap peeps out through the depressions. Those parts of the narrow vale that are irrigated by the creek and its numerous tiny tributaries are beautiful in their garb of green, while the areas that are not thus refreshed are as gray as the arid portions of the plains themselves. And that is the case everywhere among the Rockies--where no water flows over the surface the porous, sandy soil is dry and parched. The altitude of Georgetown is eight thousand four hundred and seventy-six feet. We were therefore three thousand feet higher than we had been in the morning, and had a right to expect a somewhat different avi-fauna, an expectation in which we were not disappointed.

Our initial ramble took us down the valley. The first bird noted was a familiar one--the warbling vireo, which is very abundant in Colorado in its favorite localities, where all day you may be lulled by its "silvery converse, just begun and never ended." No description of a bird so well known in both the East and the West is required, but the one seen that day gave a new performance, which seems to be worthy of more than a passing notice. Have other bird students observed it? The bird was first seen flitting about in the trees bordering the street; then it flew to its little pendent nest in the twigs. I turned my glass upon it, and, behold, there it sat in its tiny hammock singing its mercurial tune at the top of its voice. It continued its solo during the few minutes I stopped to watch it, glancing over the rim of its nest at its auditor with a pert gleam in its twinkling eyes. That was the first and only time I have ever seen a bird indulging its lyrical whim while it sat on its nest. Whether the bird was a male or a female I could not determine, but, whatever its sex, its little bosom was bubbling over with music.[11]

[11] After the foregoing was written, I chanced upon the following note in "Bird Lore" for September and October, 1901, written by a lady at Moline, Illinois, who had made an early morning visit to the haunt of a warbling vireo: "Seated on the ground, in a convenient place for watching the vireo, which was on the nest, we were soon attracted by a vireo's song. Search for the singer failed to find it, until we noted that the bird on the nest seemed to be singing. Then, as we watched, over and over again the bird was seen to lift up its head and pour out the long, rich warble--a most delicious sight and sound. Are such ways usual among birds, or did we chance to see and hear an unusual thing?"

It was soon evident that the western robins were abundant about Georgetown, as they were on the plains and among the foothills. They were principally engaged just now in feeding their young, which had already left their nests. Presently I shall have more to say about these birds. Just now I was aware of some little strangers darting about in the air, uttering a fine, querulous note, and at length descending to the ground to feast daintily on the seeds of a low plant. Here I could see them plainly with my glass, for they gave me gracious permission to go quite near them. Their backs were striped, the predominant color being brown or dark gray, while the whitish under parts were streaked with dusk, and there were yellow decorations on the wings and tails, whether the birds were at rest or in flight. When the wings were spread and in motion, the golden ornamentation gave them a filmy appearance. On the wing, the birds, as I afterwards observed, often chirped a little lay that bore a close resemblance in certain parts to the "pe-chick-o-pe" of the American goldfinch. Indeed, a number of their notes suggested that bird, as did also their manner of flight, which was quite undulatory. The birds were the pine siskins. They are very common in the Rockies, ranging from an elevation of eight thousand feet to the timber-line. This pert and dainty little bird is the same wherever found in North America, having no need of the cognomen "western" prefixed to his name when he takes it into his wise little head to make his abode in the Rocky Mountains.

CLEAR CREEK VALLEY

A scene near Georgetown. The copses in the valley are the home of white-crowned sparrows, willow thrushes, Lincoln's sparrows and Wilson's warblers; the steep, bushy acclivities are selected by the spurred and green-tailed towhees, Audubon's and Macgillivray's warblers; while the western robins, pine siskins, and broad-tailed humming-birds range all over the region. The robins and siskins make some of their most thrilling plunges over such cliffs as are shown in the picture.

The reader will perhaps recall that a flock of pine siskins were seen, two years prior, in a patch of pine scrub a short distance below Leadville, at which time I was uncertain as to their identity. Oddly enough, that was the only time I saw these birds in my first trip to Colorado, but here in the Georgetown region, only seventy-five or a hundred miles farther north, no species were more plentiful than they.

The siskins try to sing--I say "try" advisedly. It is one of the oddest bits of bird vocalization you ever heard, a wheezy little tune in the ascending scale--a kind of crescendo--which sounds as if it were produced by inhalation rather than exhalation. It is as labored as the alto strain of the clay-colored sparrow of the Kansas and Nebraska prairies, although it runs somewhat higher on the staff. The siskins seen at Georgetown moved about in good-sized flocks, feeding awhile on weed-seeds on the sunny slopes, and then wheeling with a merry chirp up to the pine-clad sides of the mountains. As they were still in the gregarious frame at Georgetown, I concluded that they had not yet begun to mate and build their nests in that locality. Afterwards I paid not a little attention to them farther up in the mountains, and saw several feeding their young, but, as their nests are built high in the pines, they are very difficult to find, or, if found, to examine. Our birdlets have superb powers of flight, and actually seem to revel in hurling themselves down a precipice or across a chasm with a recklessness that makes the observer's blood run cold. Sometimes they will dart out in the air from a steep mountain side, sing a ditty much like the goldfinch's, then circle back to their native pines on the dizzy cliff.

I must be getting back to my first ramble below Georgetown. Lured by the lyrics of the green-tailed towhee, I climbed the western acclivity a few hundred feet, but found that few birds choose such dry and eerie places for a habitat. Indeed, this was generally my experience in rambling among the mountains; the farther up the arid steeps, the fewer the birds. If you will follow a mountain brook up a sunny slope or open valley, you will be likely to find many birds; but wander away from the water courses, and you will look for them, oftentimes, in vain. The green-tailed towhees, spurred towhees, Audubon's warblers, and mountain hermit thrushes are all partial to acclivities, even very steep ones, but they do not select those that are too remote from the babbling brook to which they may conveniently resort for drinking and bathing.

A green and bushy spot a half mile below the village was the home of a number of white-crowned sparrows. None of them were seen on the plains or in the foothills; they had already migrated from the lower altitudes, and had sought their summer residences in the upper mountain valleys, where they may be found in great abundance from an elevation of eight thousand feet to copsy haunts here and there far above the timber-line hard by the fields of snow.

The white-crowns in the Georgetown valley seemed to be excessively shy, and their singing was a little too reserved to be thoroughly enjoyable, for which reason I am disposed to think that mating and nesting had not yet begun, or I should have found evidences of it, as their grassy cots on the ground and in the bushes are readily discovered. Other birds that were seen in this afternoon's ramble were Wilson's and Audubon's warblers, the spotted sandpiper, and that past-master in the art of whining, the killdeer. Another warbler's trill was heard in the thicket, but I was unable to identify the singer that evening, for he kept himself conscientiously hidden in the tanglewood. A few days later it turned out to be one of the most beautiful feathered midgets of the Rockies, Macgillivray's warbler, which was seen in a number of places, usually on bushy slopes. He and his mate often set up a great to-do by chirping and flitting about, and I spent hours in trying to find their nests, but with no other result than to wear out my patience and rubber boots. I can recall no other Colorado bird, either large or small, except the mountain jay, that made so much ado about nothing, so far as I could discover. But I love them still, on account of the beauty of their plumage and the gentle rhythm of their trills.

The next morning, chilly as the weather was--and it was cold enough to make one shiver even in bed--the western robins opened the day's concert with a splendid voluntary, waking me out of my slumbers and forcing me out of doors for an early walk. No one but a systematic ornithologist would be able to mark the difference between the eastern and western types of robins, for their manners, habits, and minstrelsy are alike, and their markings, too, so far as ordinary observation goes. The carolling of the two varieties is similar, so far as I could discern--the same cherry ringing melody, their voices having a like propensity to break into falsetto, becoming a veritable squeak, especially early in the season before their throat-harps are well tuned. With his powerful muscles and wide stretch of wing the robin is admirably adapted to the life of a mountaineer. You find him from the plains to the timber-line, sometimes even in the deepest canyons and on the most precipitous mountain sides, always the same busy, noisy, cheery body. One day I saw a robin dart like a meteor from the top of a high ridge over the cliffs to the valley below, where he alighted on a cultivated field almost as lightly as a flake of snow. He--probably she (what a trouble these pronouns are, anyway!)--gathered a mouthful of worms for his nestlings, then dashed up to the top of the ridge again, which he did, not by flying out into the air, but by keeping close up to the steep, cliffy wall, striking a rock here and twig there with his agile feet to help him in rising. The swiftness of the robin's movements about the gorges, abysses, and precipices of the mountains often inspires awe in the beholder's breast, and, on reflection, stirs him with envy. Many nests were found in the Georgetown valley, in woodsy and bushy places on the route to Gray's Peak as far as the timber-line, in the neighborhood of Boulder, in the Platte River Canyon, in South Park, and in the Blue River region beyond the Divide. Some of the nests contained eggs, others young in various stages of plumage, and still others were already deserted. For general ubiquity as a species, commend me to the American robin, whether of the eastern or western type. Wherever found he is a singer, and it is only to be regretted that--

"All will not hear thy sweet, out-pouring joy That with morn's stillness blends the voice of song, For over-anxious cares their souls employ, That else, upon thy music borne along And the light wings of heart-ascending prayer, Had learned that Heaven is pleased thy simple joys to share."

In Georgetown, Silver Plume, and other mountain towns the lovely violet-green swallow is frequently seen--a distinctly western species and one of the most richly apparelled birds of the Rockies.

It nests in all sorts of niches and crannies about the houses, often sits calmly on a telegraph wire and preens its iridescent plumes, and sometimes utters a weak and squeaky little trill, which, no doubt, passes for first-rate music in swallowdom, whatever we human critics might think of it. Before man came and settled in those valleys, the violet-greens found the crevices of rocks well enough adapted to their needs for nesting sites, but now they prefer cosey niches and crannies in human dwellings, and appear to appreciate the society of human beings.

For over a week we made Georgetown our headquarters, going off every day to the regions round about. Among my most treasured finds here was the nest of Audubon's warbler--my first. It was saddled in the crotch of a small pine a short distance up an acclivity, and was prettily roofed over with a thick network of branches and twigs. Four white, daintily speckled eggs lay in the bottom of the cup. While I was sitting in the shadow of the pine, some motion of mine caused the little owner to spring from her nest, and this led to its discovery. As she flitted about in the bushes, she uttered a sharp chip, sometimes consisting of a double note. The nest was about four feet from the ground, its walls built of grasses and weed-stems, and its concave little floor carpeted with cotton and feathers. A cosey cottage it was, fit for the little poets that erected it. Subsequently I made many long and tiresome efforts to find nests of the Audubons, but all these efforts were futile.

One enchanting day--the twenty-fourth of June--was spent in making a trip, with butterfly-net and field-glass, to Green Lake, an emerald gem set in the mountains at an altitude of ten thousand feet, a few miles from Georgetown. Before leaving the town, our first gray-headed junco for this expedition was seen. He had come to town for his breakfast, and was flitting about on the lawns and in the trees bordering the street, helping himself to such dainties as pleased his palate. It may be said here that the gray-headed juncos were observed at various places all along the way from Georgetown to Green Lake and far above that body of water. Not so with the broad-tailed hummers, which were not seen above about eight thousand five hundred feet, while the last warbling vireo of the day was seen and heard at an altitude of nine thousand feet, possibly a little more, when he decided that the air was as rare as was good for his health.

A short distance up the canyon of the west branch of Clear Creek, a new kind of flycatcher was first heard, and presently seen with my glass. He sat on a cliff or flitted from rock to bush. He uttered a sharp call, "Cheep, cheep, cheep"; his under parts were bright yellow, his upper parts yellow-olive, growing darker on the crown, and afterwards a nearer view revealed dark or dusky wings, yellowish or gray wing-bars, and yellow eye-rings. He was the western flycatcher, and bears close likeness to our eastern yellow-breasted species. Subsequently he was quite frequently met with, but never far above the altitude of Georgetown.

In the same canyon a beautiful Macgillivray's warbler was observed, and two water-ousels went dashing up the meandering stream, keeping close to the seething and roaring waters, but never stopping to sing or bid us the time of day. Very few ousels were observed in our rambles in this region, and no nests rewarded my search, whereas in the vicinity of Colorado Springs, as the reader will recall, these interesting birds were quite frequently near at hand. A mother robin holding a worm in her bill sped down the gulch with the swiftness of an arrow. We soon reached a belt of quaking asps where there were few birds. This was succeeded by a zone of pines. The green-tailed towhees did not accompany us farther in our climb than to an elevation of about nine thousand three hundred feet, but the siskins were chirping and cavorting about and above us all the way, many of them evidently having nests in the tops of the tall pines on the dizzy cliffs. Likewise the hermit thrushes were seen in suitable localities by the way, and also at the highest point we reached that day, an elevation of perhaps ten thousand five hundred feet.

While some species were, so to speak, our "companions in travel" the entire distance from the town to the lake, and others went with us only a part of the way, still other species found habitats only in the higher regions clambering far up toward the timber-line. Among these were the mountain jays, none of which were found as far down the range as Georgetown. They began to proclaim their presence by raucous calls as soon as we arrived in the vicinity of Green Lake. A family of them were hurtling about in the pine woods, allowing themselves to be inspected at short range, and filling the hollows with their uncanny calls. What a voice the mountain jay has! Nature did a queer thing when she put a "horse-fiddle" into the larynx of this bird--but it is not ours to ask the reason why, simply to study her as she is. In marked contrast with the harsh calls of these mountain hobos were the roulades of the sweet and musical ruby-crowned kinglets, which had absented themselves from the lower altitudes, but were abundant in the timber belts about ten thousand feet up the range and still higher.

On the border of the lake, among some gnarly pines, I stumbled upon a woodpecker that was entirely new to my eastern eyes--one that I had not seen in my previous touring among the heights of the Rockies. He was sedulously pursuing his vocation--a divine call, no doubt--of chiselling grubs out of the bark of the pine trees, making the chips fly, and producing at intervals that musical snare-drumming which always sets the poet to dreaming of sylvan solitudes. What was the bird? The red-naped sapsucker, a beautifully habited Chesterfield in plumes. He presently ambled up the steep mountain side, and buried himself in the pine forest, and I saw him no more, and none of his kith.

When I climbed up over a tangle of rocks to a woodsy ravine far above the lake, it seemed at first as if there were no birds in the place, that it was given up entirely to solitude; but the winged creatures were only shy and cautious for the nonce, waiting to learn something about the errand and disposition of their uninvited, or, rather, self-invited, guest, before they ventured to give him a greeting. Presently they discovered that he was not a collector, hunter, nest-robber, or ogre of any other kind, and there was the swish of wings around me, and a medley of chirps and songs filled the sequestered spot. Away up here the gray-headed juncos were trilling like warblers, and hopping about on their pine-needle carpet, creeping in and out among the rocks, hunting for tidbits. Here also was the mountain chickadee, found at this season in the heights hard by the alpine zone, singing his dulcet minor strain, "Te-te-re-e-e, te-eet," sometimes adding another "te-eet" by way of special emphasis and adornment. Oh, the sweet little piper piping only for Pan! The loneliness of the place was accentuated by the sad cadenzas of the mountain hermit thrushes. Swallows of some kind--cliff-swallows, no doubt--were silently weaving invisible filigree across the sky above the tops of the stately pines.

In the afternoon we made our way, with not a little laborious effort, to the farther end of the lake, across which a red-shafted flicker would occasionally wing its galloping flight; thence through a wilderness of large rocks and fallen pines to a beckoning ridge, where, to our surprise, another beautiful aqueous sheet greeted our vision in the valley beyond. Descending to its shores, we had still another surprise--its waters were brown instead of green. Here were two mountain lakes not more than a quarter of a mile apart, one of which was green and the other brown, each with a beauty all its own. In the brown lake near the shore there were glints of gold as the sun shone through its ripples on the rocks at the bottom. Afterwards we learned that the name of this liquid gem was Clear

Lake, and that the western branch of Clear Creek flows through it, tarrying a while to sport and dally with the sunbeams. While Green Lake was embowered in a forest of pine, its companion lay in the open sunlight, unflecked by the shadow of a tree.

At the upper end of Clear Lake we found a green, bosky and bushy corner, which formed the summer tryst of white-crowned sparrows, Wilson's warblers, and broad-tailed humming-birds, none of which could find a suitable habitat on the rocky, forest-locked shores of Green Lake. A pigeon hawk, I regretted to note, had settled among the bushes, and was watching for quarry, making the only fly in the amber of the enchanted spot. A least flycatcher flitted about in the copse some distance up a shallow runway. I trudged up the valley about a mile above Clear Lake, and found a green, open meadow, with clumps of bushes here and there, in which a few white-crowned sparrows and Wilson's warblers had taken up at least a temporary dwelling; but the wind was blowing shiveringly from the snow-capped mountains not many miles away, and there was still a wintry aspect about the vale. The cold evidently affected the birds as it did myself, for they lisped only a few bars of song in a half-hearted way. Evening was approaching, and the two travellers--the human ones, I mean--started on the trail down the valleys and canyons toward Georgetown, which they reached at dusk, tired, but thankful for the privilege of spending an idyllic day among their winged companions.

Following a wagon road, the next day, across a pass some distance below Georgetown brought us into another valley, whose green meadows and cultivated fields lay a little lower, perhaps a couple hundred feet, than the valley from which we had come. Here we found many Brewer's blackbirds, of which there were very few in the vicinity of Georgetown. They were feeding their young, some of which had already left the nest. No red-winged blackbirds had been seen in the Georgetown valley, while here there was a large colony of them, many carrying food to the bantlings in grass and bush. Otherwise there was little difference between the avi-fauna of the two valleys.

One morning I climbed the steep mountain just above Georgetown, the one that forms the divide between the two branches of Clear Creek. A western chipping sparrow sat trilling on the top of a small pine, as unafraid as the chippie that rings his silvery peals about your dooryard in the East; nor could I distinguish any difference between the minstrelsy of this westerner and his well-known cousin of Ohio. He dexterously caught an insect on the wing, having learned that trick, perhaps, from his neighbor, the little western flycatcher, which also lived on the slope. Hermit thrushes, Audubon's warblers, and warbling vireos dwelt on the lower part of the acclivity. When I climbed far up the steep wall, scarcely able to cling to its gravelly surface, I found very few birds; only a flycatcher and an Audubon's warbler, while below me the hermit thrushes were chanting a sacred oratorio in the pine woods.

On another day the train bore us around the famous "Loop" to Silver Plume. In the beautiful pine grove at the terminus of the railway there were many birds--siskins, chipping sparrows, western robins and ruby-crowned kinglets; and they were making the place vocal with melody, until I began to inspect them with my glass, when they suddenly lapsed into a silence that was as trying as it was profound. By and by, discretion having had her perfect work, they metaphorically came out of their shells and permitted an inspection. Above the railway I saw one of the few birds of my entire Rocky Mountain outing that I was unable to identify. That little feathered Sphinx--what could he have been? To quote from my note-book, "His song, as he sits quietly on a twig in a pine tree, is a rich gurgling trill, slightly like that of a house-wren, but fuller and more melodious, with an air about it that makes me feel almost like writing a poem. The bird is in plain view before me, and I may watch him either with or without my glass; he has a short, conical bill; his upper parts are gray or olive-gray; cervical patch of a greenish tinge; under parts whitish, spotted with dusk or brown. The bill is white or horn-color, and is quite heavy, I should say heavier than that of any sparrow I know. The bird continued to sing for a long time and at frequent intervals, not even stopping when the engine near at hand blew off steam, although he turned his head and looked a little startled." I saw this species nowhere else in my Colorado rambles, and can find no description in the systematic manuals that helps to clear up the mystery, and so an avis incognita he must remain for the present.

Has mention been made of a few house-finches that were seen in Georgetown? Only a few, however, for they prefer the towns and cities of the plain. Several house-wrens were also seen in the vicinity of the Georgetown Loop as well as elsewhere in the valley. The "Loop," although a monumental work of human genius and daring, has its peculiar attractions for the student of natural history, for in the canyon itself, which is somewhat open and not without bushy haunts, and on the precipitous mountain sides, a few birds set up their Lares and Penates, and mingle their songs of domestic felicity with the roar of the torrent and the passing trains. Darting like zigzag lightning about the cliffs, the broad-tailed humming-bird cuts the air with his sharp, defiant buzz, until you exclaim with the poet:

"Is it a monster bee, Or is it a midget bird, Or yet an air-born mystery That now yon marigold has stirred?"

Among the birds that dwell on the steep mountain sides above the "Loop" hollow are the melodious green-tailed towhees, lisping their chansons of good-will to breeze and torrent, while in the copse of asps in the hollow itself the warbling vireo and the western flycatcher hold sway, the former rehearsing his recitative all the day long, and the latter chirping his protest at every human intrusion. On a pine-clad shelf between the second fold of the "Loop" and what is known as the "Great Fill" I settled (at least, to my own satisfaction) a long-disputed point in regard to the vocalization of the mountain hermit thrush. Again and again I had noticed a peculiarity about the hermit's minstrelsy--whenever the music reached my ear, it came in two runs, the first quite high in the scale, the second perhaps an octave lower. For a long time I supposed that two thrushes were singing responsively, but here at the "Loop," after listening for a couple of hours, it occurred to me as improbable that there would invariably be a respondent when a thrush lifted up his voice in song. Surely there would sometimes, at least, be solo singing in the thrush realm. And so the conclusion was forced upon me that both strains emanated from the same throat, that each vocalist was its own respondent. It was worth while to clamber laboriously about the "Loop" to settle a point like that--at all events, it was worth while for one admirer of the birds.

HO! FOR GRAY'S PEAK!

By the uninitiated it may be regarded simply as fun and pastime to climb a mountain whose summit soars into cloudland; in reality it is serious business, not necessarily accompanied with great danger, but always accomplished by laborious effort. However, it is better for the clamberer to look upon his undertaking as play rather than work. Should he come to feel that it is actual toil, he might soon weary of a task engaged in so largely for its own sake, and decide to expend his time and energy in something that would "pay better." Moreover, if he is impelled by a hobby--ornithology, for instance--in addition to the mere love of mountaineering, he will find that something very near akin to wings has been annexed to the climbing gear of which he is naturally possessed.

The morning of June 27 saw my youthful companion and myself mounted each upon a shaggy burro, scrambling up the steep hill above Georgetown, en route for Gray's Peak, the ascent of which was the chief goal of our ambition in coming to the Rockies on the present expedition. The distance from Georgetown to the summit of this peak is fourteen miles, and the crest itself is fourteen thousand four hundred and forty-one feet above sea-level, almost three hundred feet higher than Pike's Peak, and cannot be scaled by means of a cog-wheel railway or any other contrivance that uses steam or electricity as a motor. Indeed, the only motor available at the time of our ascent--that is, for the final climb--was "shank's horses," very useful and mostly safe, even if a little plebeian. We had been wise enough not to plunge at once among the heights, having spent almost a week rambling over the plains, mesas, foothills, and lower ranges, then had been occupied for five or six days more in exploring the valleys and mountain sides in the vicinity of Georgetown, and thus, by gradually approaching them, we had become inured to "roughing it" in the higher altitudes when we reached them, and suffered no ill effects from the rarefied atmosphere.

We passed the famous "Georgetown Loop," crept at a snail's pace--for that is the natural gait of the burro--through the town of Silver Plume, and pursued our leisurely journey toward the beckoning, snow-clad heights beyond. No, we did not hurry, for two reasons: First, our little four-footers would not or could not quicken their pace, urge them as we would; second, we desired to name all the birds along the route, and that "without a gun," as Emerson mercifully enjoins.

Have you ever ridden a burro? Have you ever been astride of an old one, a hirsute, unkempt, snail-paced, obstinate one, which thinks he knows better what gait he ought to assume than you do?

If you have not, I venture to suggest modestly that your education and moral discipline are not quite complete. The pair which we had hired were slow and headstrong enough to develop the patience of Job in a most satisfactory way, and to test it, too. They were as homely as the proverbial "mud fence" is supposed to be. Never having seen a fence of that kind, I speak with some degree of caution, not wanting to cast any disparagement upon something of which I have so little knowledge. If our long-eared companions had ever seen a curry-comb, it must have been in the days of Noah. You see, we were "tenderfoots," as far as having had any experience with burros was concerned, or we might have selected a more sprightly pair for our fellow-pilgrims. A fine picture, fit for the camera or the artist's brush, we presented as we crept with the speed of a tortoise along the steep mountain roads and trails. Our "jacks," as Messrs. Longears are called colloquially, were not lazy--oh, no! they were simply averse to leaving home! Their domestic ties were so strong they bound them with cords of steel and hooks of iron to stall and stable-yard! The thought of forsaking friends and kindred even for only a few days wrung their loving hearts with anguish! No wonder we had a delicate and pathetic task on hand when we attempted to start our caravan up the mountain road. From side to side the gentle animals wabbled, their load of grief weighing them down tenfold more than the loads on their backs, and times without count they were prompted to veer about and "turn again home."

Much labor and time and patience were expended in persuading our steeds to crawl up the hill, but I am delighted to say that no profane history was quoted, as we were a strictly moral crowd. At length we arrived in state at the village of Silver Plume. Canter into the town like a gang of border ruffians we did not; we entered deliberately, as became a dignified company of travellers. But here a new difficulty confronted us, stared us blankly in the face. Our little charges could not be convinced that there was any occasion for going farther than the town. They seemed to have conscientious scruples about the matter; so they stopped without any invitation from their riders, sidled off, turned in toward the residences, stores, groceries, shoe-shops, drugstores, barns, and even the saloons, the while the idlers on the streets and the small boys were gawking at us, smiling in a half-suppressed way, and making quaint remarks in which we could see no wisdom nor humor. We had not come into the town, like Don Quixote and Sancho Panza, merely to furnish the villagers amusement. Applying our canes and straps forcibly to the haunches and rumps of our burros only seemed to embarrass the poor creatures, for you can readily see how they would reason the matter out from their own premises: If they were to go no farther, as had been decided by themselves, why should their riders belabor them in that merciless way? For downright dialectics commend me to the Rocky Mountain burro.

Finally a providence in the shape of two small boys came to our rescue, and in a most interesting and effective way. Seeing the predicament we were in, and appreciating the gravity of the situation, those nimble-witted lads picked up a couple of clubs from the street, and, getting in the rear of our champing steeds, began to pound them over the haunches. For small boys they delivered sturdy blows. Now, if there is anything that will make a burro move dexterously out of his tracks, it is to get behind him with a club and beat a steady tattoo on his hams and legs. No sooner did the boys begin to apply their clubs in good earnest than our burros began to print tracks in quick succession on the dusty road, and we went gayly through the town, the lads making a merry din with their shouts and whacks, mingled with the patter of hoofs on the street. It was so dramatic that even the women came to their doors to witness the pageant. We tried not to laugh, and so did the delicately mannered spectators, but I suspect that a good deal of laughing was done on the sly, in spite of the canons of etiquette.

At length the obliging lads became a little too accommodating. They used their persuasives upon the donkeys so vigorously that they--the donkeys--started off on a lope, a sort of awkward, lop-sided gallop. Now, if there is anything that is beyond the ability of Master Jack, especially if he is old, it is to canter and at the same time preserve his equilibrium. It is evident that he is not built to make a rocking-chair of his back bone. So a little comedy was enacted, all involuntary on the part of the dramatis person? Suddenly Turpentine--that was the name of the little gray burro ridden by my boy companion--took a header, sending his youthful rider sprawling to the ground, where he did not remain a moment longer than good manners demanded. Fortunately he succeeded in disengaging his feet from the stirrups and directing his movements in such a way that the animal did not fall upon him. But poor Turpentine, what of him? He tumbled clean over his head upon his back, and I want to confess in all candor that one of the most instructive and interesting "animal pictures" I have ever seen, including those done by Landseer, Rosa Bonheur, and Ernest Thompson Seton, was that little iron-gray, long-eared donkey lying on his back on the street and clawing the air with his hoofs. And he clawed fast, too--fairly sawed the air. For once in his life Turpentine, the snail paced, was in a hurry; for once he moved with more celerity than grace. It threw us into spasms of laughter to see him exert himself so vigorously to reverse his position--to get his feet down and his back up. A cat could not have done it with more celerity. You never would have believed him capable of putting so much vim and vigor into his easy-going personality. After chopping the air with his hoofs for a second or two, he succeeded in righting himself, and was on his feet in less time than it takes to tell it. There he stood, as meek as Mary's lamb, trying to look as if he had never turned an undignified somersault in all his tranquil life.

We started on our journey again, and presently, to our intense relief, reached the border of the town, thanked the lads who had expedited our march along the street, and proceeded on our way up the valley. We soon settled down to taking our burros philosophically, and erelong they were going calmly on the even tenor of their way, and afterwards we had little trouble with them, and actually became quite attached to the gentle creatures before our joint pilgrimage drew to an end.

It is time to pass from quadrupeds to bipeds. While our feathered friends were not so abundant in the wilder regions as we might have wished, still we had almost constant avian companionship along the way. The warbling vireos were especially plentiful, and in full tune, making a silvery trail of song beside the dusty road. We had them at our elbow as far as Graymont, where we made a sharp detour from the open valley, and clambered along a steep mountain side, with a deep, wooded gorge below us. Here the vireos suddenly decided that they could escort us no farther, as they had no taste for crepuscular canyons and alpine heights. Not a vireo was seen above Graymont, which has an altitude of nearly ten thousand feet. We left them singing in the valley as we turned from it, and did not hear them again until we came back to Graymont.

Almost the same may be said of the broad-tailed humming-birds, whose insect-like buzzing we heard at frequent intervals along the route to a shoulder of the mountain a little above Graymont, when it suddenly ceased and was heard no more until we returned to the same spot a few days later. House-wrens, willow thrushes, Brewer's blackbirds, and long-crested jays were also last seen at Graymont, which seemed to be a kind of territorial limit for a number of species.

However, several species--as species, of course, not as

individuals--convoyed us all the way from Georgetown to the timber-line and, in some instances, beyond. Let me call the roll of these faithful "steadies": Mountain hermit thrushes, gray-headed juncos, red-shafted flickers, pine siskins, western robins, Audubon's and Wilson's warblers, mountain bluebirds and white-crowned sparrows. Of course, it must be borne in mind that these birds were not seen everywhere along the upward journey, simply in their favorite habitats. The deep, pine-shadowed gorges were avoided by the warblers and white-crowned sparrows, whilst every open, sunlit, and bushy spot or bosky glen was enlivened by a contingent of these merry minnesingers. One little bird added to our list in the gorge above Graymont was the mountain chickadee, which was found thereafter up to the timber-line.

It was sometime in the afternoon when we reached Graymont, which we found to be no "mount" at all, as we had expected, but a hamlet, now mostly deserted, in a narrow valley in sight of several gray mountains looming in the distance. Straight up the valley were some snow-mantled peaks, but none of them was Gray's; they did not beckon to us from the right direction. From the upper part of the hamlet, looking to our left, we saw a frowning, snow-clad ridge towering like an angry giant in the air, and we cried simultaneously, "Gray's Peak!" The terrific aspect of that mountain sent a momentary shiver through our veins as we thought of scaling it without a guide. We were in error, as we afterwards found, for the mountain was Torrey's Peak, not Gray's, which is not visible from Graymont, being hidden by two intervening elevations, Mount Kelso and Torrey's Peak. There are several points about a mile above Graymont from which Gray's serene peak is visible, but of this we were not aware until on our return trip, when we had learned to recognize him by his calm and magisterial aspect.

As evening drew on, and the westering sun fell below the ridges, and the shadows deepened in the gorges, making them doubly weird, we began to feel very lonely, and, to add to our misgivings, we were uncertain of our way. The prospect of having to spend a cold night out of doors in a solitary place like this was not very refreshing, I am free to confess, much as one might desire to proclaim himself a brave man. Presently our eyes were gladdened by the sight of a miner's shack just across the hollow, perhaps the one for which we were anxiously looking. A man at Graymont had told us about a miner up this way, saying he was a "nice man" and would no doubt give us accommodation for the night. I crossed the narrow foot-bridge that spanned the booming torrent, and found the miner at home. Would he give two way-worn travelers a place to sleep beneath his roof? We had brought plenty of food and some blankets with us, and all we required was four walls around us and a roof over our heads. Yes, he replied, we were welcome to such accommodation as he had, and he could even give us a bed, though it "wasn't very stylish." Those were among the sweetest and most musical words that ever fell on my ear.

Having tethered our burros in a grassy cove on the mountain side, and cooked our supper in the gloaming among some rocks by the bank of the brawling stream, we turned into the cabin for the night, more than grateful for a shelter from the chill winds scurrying down from the snow-capped mountains. The shack nestled at the foot of Mount Kelso, which we had also mistaken for Gray's Peak. As we sat by the light of a tallow candle, beguiling the evening with conversation, the miner told us that the mountain jays, colloquially called "camp robbers," were common around his cabin, especially in winter; but familiar as they were, he had never been able to find a nest. The one thing about which they insist on the utmost privacy is their nesting places. My friend also told me that a couple of gray squirrels made the woods around his camp their home. The jays would frequently carry morsels of food up to the branches of the pines, and stow them in some crevice for future use, whereupon the squirrels, always on the lookout for their own interests, would scuttle up the tree and steal the hidden provender, eating it with many a chuckle of self-congratulation.

Had not the weather turned so cold during the night, we might have slept quite comfortably in the miner's shack, but I must confess that, though it was the twenty-eighth of June and I had a small mountain of cover over me, I shivered a good deal toward morning. An hour or so after daylight four or five mountain jays came to the cabin for their breakfast, flitting to the ground and greedily devouring such tidbits as they could find. They were not in the least shy. But where were their nests? That was the question that most deeply interested me. During the next few days I made many a long and toilsome search for them in the woods and ravines and on the steep mountain sides, but none of the birds invited me to their houses. These birds know how to keep a secret. Anything but feathered Apollos, they have a kind of ghoulish aspect, making you think of the apparitional as they move in their noiseless way among the shadowing pines. There is a look in their dark, deep-set eyes and about their thick, clumpy heads which gives you a feeling that they might be equal to any imaginable act of cruelty. Yet I cannot say I dislike these mountain roustabouts, for some of their talk among themselves is very tender and affectionate, proving that, "whatever brawls disturb the street," there are love and concord in jay household circles. That surely is a virtue to be commended, and cannot be claimed for every family, either avian or human.

At 4.30 that morning I crept out of bed and climbed far up one of the mountain sides--this was before the jays came to the cabin. The wind blew so icy from the snow-clad heights that I was only too glad to wear woollen gloves and pin a bandanna handkerchief around my neck, besides buttoning up my coat collar. Even then I shivered. But would you believe it? The mosquitoes were as lively and active as if a balmy breeze were blowing from Arcady, puncturing me wherever they could find a vulnerable spot, and even thrusting their sabres through my thick woollen gloves into the flesh. They must be extremely hardy insects, for I am sure such arctic weather would send the mosquitoes of our lower altitudes into their winter hiding-places. People who think there are no mosquitoes in the Rockies are reckoning without their hosts. In many places they assaulted us by the myriad until life among them became intolerable, and some were found even in the neighborhood of perpetual snow.

Raw as the morning was, the hermit thrushes, mountain chickadees, Audubon's warblers, gray-headed juncos, and ruby-crowned kinglets were giving a lively rehearsal. How shy they were! They preferred being heard, not seen. Unexpectedly I found a hermit thrush's nest set in plain sight in a pine bush. One would have thought so shy a bird would make some attempt at concealment. It was a well-constructed domicile, composed of grass, twigs, and moss, but without mortar. The shy owner was nowhere to be seen, nor did she make any outcry, even though I stood for some minutes close to her nest. What stolidity the mountain birds display! You could actually rob the nests of some of them without wringing a chirp from them. On two later visits to the place I found Madame Thrush on her nest, where she sat until I came quite close, when she silently flitted away and ensconced herself among the pines, never chirping a syllable of protest or fear. In the bottom of the pretty crib lay four deep-blue eggs. Afterwards I found one more hermit's nest, which was just in process of construction. In this case, as in the first, no effort was made at concealment, the nest being placed in the crotch of a quaking asp a rod or so above the trail, from which it could be plainly seen. The little madame was carrying a load of timbers to her cottage as we went down the trail, and sat in the nest moulding and putting her material in place as I climbed up the steep bank to inspect her work. Then she flew away, making no demonstration while I examined the nest.

Having eaten our breakfast at the miner's cabin, my youthful companion and I mounted our "gayly caparisoned steeds," and resumed our journey toward Gray's Peak. The birds just mentioned greeted us with their salvos as we crept along. It was not until we had almost reached the timber-line that Gray's Peak loomed in sight, solemn and majestic, photographed against the cobalt sky, with its companion-piece, Torrey's Peak, standing sullen beside it. The twin peaks were pointed out to us by another miner whom we met at his shack just a little below the timber-line, and who obligingly gave us permission to "bunk" in one of the cabins of what is known as "Stephen's mine," which is now abandoned--or was at the time of our visit. Near the timber-line, where the valley opens to the sunlight, we found a mountain bluebird flitting about some old, deserted buildings, but, strangely enough, this was the last time we saw him, although we looked for him again and again. Nor did we see another mountain blue in this alpine eyrie.

Our burros were tethered for the day in a grassy hollow, our effects stowed away in the cabin aforesaid, which we had leased for a few days; then, with luncheon strapped over our shoulders and butterfly net and field-glass in hand, we started happily up the valley afoot toward the summit of our aspirations, Gray's Peak, rising fourteen thousand four hundred and forty-one feet above the level of the sea. In some scrubby pine bushes above timber-line several Audubon's warblers were flitting and singing, living hard by the white fields of snow. Still farther up the hollow Wilson's warblers were trilling blithely, proclaiming themselves yet more venturesome than their gorgeous cousins, the Audubons. There is reason for this difference, for Wilson's warblers nest in willows and other bushes which thrive on higher ground and nearer the snowy zone than do the pines to which Audubon's warblers are especially attached. At all events, Sylvania pusilla was one of the two species which accompanied us all the way from Georgetown to the foot of Gray's Peak, giving us a kind of "personally conducted" journey.

Our other brave escorts were the white-crowned sparrows, which pursued the narrowing valleys until they were merged into the snowy gorges that rive the sides of the towering twin peaks. In the arctic gulches the scrubby copses came to an end, and therefore the white-crowns ascended no higher, for they are, in a pre-eminent sense, "birds of the bush." Subsequently I found them as far up the sides of Mount Kelso as the thickets extended, which was hundreds of feet higher than the snow-bound gorges just mentioned, for Kelso receives more sunshine than his taller companions, particularly on his eastern side. Brave birds are these handsome and musical sparrows. It was interesting to see them hopping about on the snow-fields, picking up dainties from the white crystals. How lyrical they were in this upper mountain valley! As has been said, for some unaccountable reason the white-crowns in the vicinity of Georgetown were quite chary of their music. Not so those that dwelt in the valley below Gray's and Torrey's peaks, for there they trilled their melodious measures with a richness and abandon that were enchanting.

On reaching the snow-belt, though still a little below the limit of copsy growths, we saw our first pipits, which, it will be remembered, I had encountered on the summit of Pike's Peak two years before. In our climb up Gray's Peak we found the pipit realm and that of the white-crowned sparrows slightly overlapping. As soon, however, as we began the steep climb above the matted copses, the white-crowns disappeared and the pipits grew more abundant. At frequent intervals these birds would suddenly start up from the ground, utter their protesting "Te-cheer! te-cheer!" and hurl themselves recklessly across a snowy gulch, or dart high into the air and let their semi-musical calls drop and dribble from the turquoise depths of the sky. Did the pipits accompany you to the summit of the peak? I half regret to admit that they did not, but ceased to appear a good while before the summit was attained. This is all the more remarkable when it is remembered that these birds were extremely abundant on the crest of Pike's Peak, where they behaved in a "very-much-at-home" way.

However, there was ample compensation in the ascent of Gray's Peak. As we clambered up the steep and rugged side of the mountain, sometimes wading snow up to our knees, then making a short cut straight up the acclivity to avoid the snow-banks, unable to follow the trail a large part of the way, we were suddenly made aware of the presence of another fearless feathered comrade. With a chirp that was the very quintessence of good cheer and lightness of heart, he hopped about on the snow, picking dainties from his immaculate tablecloth, and permitting us to approach him quite close before he thought it worth while to take to wing. We were happy indeed to meet so companionable a little friend, one that, amid these lonely and awe-inspiring heights, seemed to feel so much at ease and exhibited so confiding a disposition. Was it fancy or was it really true? He appeared to be giving us a hospitable welcome to his alpine home, telling us we might venture upward into cloudland or skyland without peril; then, to make good his assurance, he mounted upward on resilient wings to prove how little danger there was. We were doubly glad for our little seer, for just then we needed someone to "prophesy smooth things" to us. The bird was the brown-capped leucosticte or rosy finch. Thus far I have used the singular number, but the plural would have been more accurate, for there were many of these finches on the acclivity and summit, all of them in a most cheerful mood, their good will and cordial welcome giving us a pleasant feeling of comradery as we journeyed together up the mountain side.

Our climb up Gray's Peak was a somewhat memorable event in

our experience, and I am disposed to dwell upon it. The valley which we had followed terminates in a deep gorge, filled with drift snow the year round, no doubt, and wedging itself between Gray's and Torrey's shoulders and peaks. Here the melting snows form the head waters of Clear Creek, whose sinuous course we had followed by rail, foot, and burro from the city of Denver.

The trail, leaving the ravine, meandered up a shoulder of the mountain, wheeled to the left and crept along a ridge, with some fine, blood-curdling abysses on the eastern side; then went zigzagging back and forth on the precipitous wall of Gray's titanic mount, until at last, with a long pull and a strong pull, it scaled the backbone of the ridge. All this, however, is much more easily told than done. Later in the season, when the trail is clear of snow-drifts, sure-footed horses and burros are ridden to the summit; but we were too early to follow the trail even on foot. Indeed, many persons familiar with the mountains had declared that we could not reach the top so early in the season, on account of the large snow-banks that still covered the trail. Even the old miner, who in the valley below pointed out the peak to us, expressed grave doubts about the success and wisdom of our undertaking. "See!" he said, "the trail's covered with snow in many places on the mountain side. I'm afraid you can't reach the top, sir." I did not see as clearly as he did, but said nothing aloud. In my mind I shouted, "Excelsior!" and then added, mentally, of course, "Faint heart never won fair lady or fairer mountain's crest--hurrah for the peak!" I simply felt that if there were birds and butterflies on that sky-aspiring tower, I must see them. The die was cast; we had come to Colorado expressly to climb Gray's Peak, and climb it we would, or have some good reason to give for not doing so.

And now we were making the attempt. We had scarcely reached the mountain's shoulder before we were obliged to wade snow. For quite a distance we were able to creep along the edge of the trail, or skirt the snow-beds by making short detours, and then returning to the trail; but by and by we came to a wide, gleaming snow-field that stretched right athwart our path and brought us to a standstill with the exclamation, "What shall we do now?" Having already sunk a number of times into the snow over our boot-tops, we felt that it would not be safe to venture across so large an area of soft and treacherous crystals melting in the afternoon sun and only slightly covering we knew not what deep gorges. In some places we had been able to walk on the top of the snow, but elsewhere it was quite soft, and we could hear the gurgling of water underneath, and sometimes it sounded a little more sepulchral than we liked. Looking far up the acclivity, we saw still larger snow-fields obliterating the trail. "We can never cross those snow-fields," one of us declared, a good deal of doubt in his tones. A moment's reflection followed, and then the other exclaimed stoutly, "Let us climb straight up, then!" To which his companion replied, "All right, little Corporal! Beyond the Alps lies Italy!"

Over rocks and stones and stretches of gravel, sometimes loose, sometimes solid, we clambered, half the time on all fours, skirting the snow-fields that lay in our unblazed pathway; on and up, each cheering the other at frequent intervals by crying lustily, "We can make it! We can make it!" ever and anon throwing ourselves on the rocks to recover our breath and rest our aching limbs; on and up we scrambled and crept, like ants on a wall, until at length, reaching the ridge at the left a little below the top, we again struck the trail, when we stopped a few minutes to catch breath, made one more mighty effort, and, behold! we stood on Gray's summit, looking down triumphantly at the world crouching at our feet. Never before had we felt so much like Jupiter on Olympus.

GRAY'S AND TORREY'S PEAKS

Gray's to the left, Torrey's to the right. As the lookout of the photographer was nearer Torrey's than Gray's, the former appears the higher in the picture, while the reverse is really the case. The trail winds through a ravine at the right of the ridge in front; then creeps along the farther side of the ridge above the gorge at Torrey's base; comes to the crest of the ridge pretty well toward the left; then crawls and zigzags back and forth along the titanic wall of Gray's to the summit. In the vale, where some of the head waters of Clear Creek will be seen, the white-crowned sparrows and Wilson's warblers find homes. A little before the ascent of the ridge begins, the first pipits are seen; thence the clamberer has pipit company to the point where the ridge joins the main bulk of the mountain. Here the pipits stop, and the first leucostictes are noted, which, chirping cheerily all the way, escort the traveller to the summit.

In making the ascent, some persons, even among those who ride, become sick; others suffer with bleeding at the nose, and others are so overcome with exhaustion and weakness that they cannot enjoy the superb panorama spread out before them. However you may account for it, my youthful comrade and I, in spite of our arduous climb, were in excellent physical condition when we reached our goal, suffering no pain whatever in eyes, head, or lungs. The bracing air, rare as it was, soon exhilarated us, our temporary weariness disappeared, and we were in the best of trim for scouring the summit, pursuing our natural history hobbies, and revelling in the inspiring cyclorama that Nature had reared for our delectation.

My pen falters when I think of describing the scene that broke upon our vision. I sigh and wish the task were done. The summit itself is a narrow ridge on which you may stand and look down the declivities on both sides, scarcely having to step out of your tracks to do so. It is quite different from the top of Pike's Peak, which is a comparatively level plateau several acres in extent, carpeted, if one may so speak, with immense granite rocks piled upon one another or laid side by side in semi-systematic order; whereas Gray's, as has been said, is a narrow ridge, composed chiefly of comparatively small stones, with a sprinkling of good-sized boulders. The finer rocks give the impression of having been ground down by crushing and attrition to their present dimensions in the far-away, prehistoric ages.

A short distance to the northwest frowned Torrey's Peak, Gray's companion-piece, the twain being connected by a ridge which dips in an arc perhaps a hundred feet below the summits. The ridge was covered with a deep drift of snow, looking as frigid and unyielding as a scene in the arctic regions. Torrey's is only a few feet lower than Gray's--one of my books says five. Mention has been made of its forbidding aspect. It is indeed one of the most ferocious-looking mountains in the Rockies, its crown pointed and grim, helmeted with snow, its sides, especially east and north, seamed and ridged and jagged, the gorges filled with snow, the beetling cliffs jutting dark and threatening, bearing huge drifts upon their shoulders. Torrey's Peak actually seemed to be calling over to us like some boastful Hercules, "Ah, ha! you have climbed my mild-tempered brother, but I dare you to climb me!" For reasons of our own we declined the challenge.

The panorama from Gray's Peak is one to inspire awe and dwell forever in the memory, an alpine wonderland indeed and in truth. To the north, northwest, and west there stretches, as far as the eye can reach, a vast wilderness of snowy peaks and ranges, many of them with a rosy glow in the sunshine, tier upon tier, terrace above terrace, here in serried ranks, there in isolated grandeur, some just beyond the dividing canyons, others fifty, sixty, a hundred miles away, cyclopean, majestic, infinite. Far to the north, Long's Peak lifts his seamed and hoary pyramid, almost as high as the crest on which we are standing; in the west rise that famous triad of peaks, Harvard, Yale, and Princeton, their fanelike towers, sketched against the sky, disputing the palm with old Gray himself; while a hundred miles to the south Pike's Peak stands solitary and smiling in the sun, seeming to say, "I am sufficient unto myself!" Between our viewpoint and the last-named mountain lies South Park, like a paradise of green immured by guardian walls of rock and snow, and far to the east, beyond the billowing ranges, white, gray, and green, stretch the limitless plains, vanishing in the hazy distance. In such surroundings one's breast throbs and swells with the thought of Nature's omnipotence.

PANORAMA FROM GRAY'S PEAK--NORTHWEST

The picture includes the northern spur of Gray's Peak, with the dismantled signal station on its crest. The main ridge of the peak extends out to the left of the signal station. The summit is so situated as to be exposed to the sun the greater part of the day; hence, although it is the highest point in the region, there is less snow upon it in summer than upon many of the surrounding elevations. Looking northwest from the signal station, the eye falls upon a wilderness of snow-clad peaks and ranges, some standing in serried ranks, others in picturesque disorder. It is truly an arctic scene, summer or winter. Yet it is the summer home of the brown-capped leucosticte and the white-tailed ptarmigan, which range in happy freedom over the upper story of our country.

The summit of Gray's Peak is a favorable viewpoint from which to study the complexion, the idiosyncrasies, if you please, of individual mountains, each of which seems to have a personality of its own. Here is Gray's Peak itself, calm, smiling, good-natured as a summer morning; yonder is Torrey's, next-door neighbor, cruel, relentless, defiant, always threatening with cyclone or tornado, or forging the thunder-bolts of Vulcan. Some mountains appear grand and dignified, others look like spitfires. On one side some bear smooth and green slopes almost to the top, while the other is scarred, craggy, and precipitous.

The day was serene and beautiful, the sky a deep indigo, unflecked with clouds, save a few filmy wracks here and there, and the breeze as balmy as that of a May morning in my native State. So quiet was the alpine solitude that on all sides we could hear the solemn roar of the streams in the ravines hundreds of feet below, some of them in one key and some in another, making almost a symphony. For several hours we tarried, held by a spell. "But you have forgotten your ornithology!" some one reminds me. No one could blame me if I had. Such, however, is not the case, for ornithology, like the poor, is never far from some of us. The genial little optimists that had been hopping about on the snow on the declivities had acted as our cicerones clear to the summit, and some of them remained there while we tarried. Indeed the leucostictes were quite plentiful on the mountain's brow. Several perched on the dismantled walls of the abandoned government building on the summit, called cheerily, then wheeled about over the crest, darted out and went careering over the gulches with perfect aplomb, while we watched them with envious eyes, wishing we too had wings like a leucosticte, not that we "might fly away," as the Psalmist longed to do, but that we might scale the mountains at our own sweet will. The favorite occupation of our little comrades, besides flying, was hopping about on the snow and picking up dainties that were evidently palatable. Afterwards we examined the snow, and found several kinds of small beetles and other insects creeping up through it or about on its surface. Without doubt these were leucosticte's choice morsels. Thus Nature spreads her table everywhere with loving care for her feathered children. The general habits of the rosy finches are elsewhere depicted in this volume. It only remains to be said that they were much more abundant and familiar on Gray's Peak than on Pike's Peak,--that is, at the time of my respective visits to those summits.

To omit all mention of the butterflies seen on this trip would be proof of avian monomania with a vengeance. The lad who was with me found a number of individuals of two species zigzagging over the summit, and occasionally settling upon the rocks right by the fields of snow. What kind of nectar they sipped I know not, for there were no flowers or verdure on the heights. They were the Painted Lady or Thistle Butterfly (Pyrameis cardui) and the Western White (Pieris occidentalis). He captured an individual of the latter species with his net, and to-day it graces his collection, a memento of a hard but glorious climb. The descent of the mountain was laborious and protracted, including some floundering in the snow, but was accomplished without accident. A warm supper in the miner's shack which we had leased prepared us for the restful slumbers of the night.

Although the weather was so cold that a thin coating of ice was formed on still water out of doors, the next morning the white-crowned sparrows were singing their sonatas long before dawn, and when at peep of day I stepped outside, they were flitting about the cabins as if in search of their breakfast. The evening before, I left the stable-door open while I went to bring the burros up from their grazing plat. When I returned with the animals, a white-crown flew out of the building just as I stepped into the entrance, almost fluttering against my feet, and chirping sharply at what he seemed to think a narrow escape. He had doubtless gone into the stable on a foraging expedition.

The day was spent in exploring the valley and steep mountain sides. A robin's nest was found a little below the timber-line on the slope of Mount Kelso. In the woods a short distance farther down, a gray-headed junco's nest was discovered after a good deal of patient waiting. A female was preening her feathers on a small pine-tree, a sure sign that she had recently come from brooding her eggs. Presently she began to flit about from the tree to the ground and back again, making many feints and starts, which proved that she was embarrassed by my espionage; but at last she disappeared and did not return. With quickened pulse I approached the place where I had last seen her. It was not long before she flew up with a nervous chirp, revealing a pretty domicile under a roof of green grass, with four daintily speckled eggs on the concave floor. I noticed especially that the doorway of the tiny cottage was open toward the morning sun.

At the timber-line there were ruby-crowned kinglets, mountain chickadees, and gray-headed juncos, while far above this wavering boundary a pair of red-shafted flickers were observed ambling about among the bushes and watching me as intently as I was watching them. I climbed far up the side of Mount Kelso, then around its rocky shoulder, following an old trail that led to several abandoned silver mines, but no new birds rewarded my toilsome quest, although I was pleased to learn that the pipits and leucostictes did not give the "go-by" to this grand old mountain, but performed their thrilling calisthenics in the air about its slopes and ravines with as much grace as they did on the loftier mountain peaks the day before. A beautiful fox and three cubs were seen among the large stones, and many mountain rats and a sly mink went scuttling about over the rocks.

On the morning of June 30 the white-crowns, as usual, were chanting their litanies long before day broke. We left the enchanting valley that morning, the trills of the white-crowns ringing in the alpenglow like a sad farewell, as if they felt that we should never meet again. On our way down the winding road we frequently turned to gaze with longing eyes upon the snowy summits of the twin peaks, Gray's all asmile in the sunshine, and Torrey's--or did we only imagine it?--relenting a little now that he was looking upon us for the last time. Did the mountains and the white-crowns call after us, "Auf wiedersehen!" or was that only imagination too?

PLEASANT OUTINGS

One of our pleasantest trips was taken up South Platte Canyon, across South Park, and over the range to Breckenridge. The town lies in the valley of the Blue River, the famous Ten Mile Range, with its numerous peaks and bold and rugged contour, standing sentinel on the west. Here we found many birds, but as few of them were new, I need not stop to enter into special detail.

At the border of the town I found my first green-tailed towhee's nest, which will be described in the last chapter. A pair of mountain bluebirds had snuggled their nest in a cranny of one of the cottages, and an entire family of blues were found on the pine-clad slope beyond the stream; white-crowned sparrows were plentiful in the copses and far up the bushy ravines and mountain sides; western chippies rang their silvery peals; violet-green swallows wove their invisible fabrics overhead; juncos and Audubon's warblers proclaimed their presence in many a remote ingle by their little trills; and Brewer's blackbirds "chacked" their remonstrance at every intrusion into their demesnes; while in many a woodsy or bushy spot the long-crested jays rent the air with their raucous outcries; nor were the broad-tailed hummers wanting on this side of the range, and of course their saucy buzzing was heard wherever they darted through the air.

An entire day was spent in ascending and descending Peak Number Eight, one of the boldest of the jutting crags of the Ten Mile Range; otherwise it is called Tillie Ann, in honor of the first white woman known to scale its steep and rugged wall to the summit. She must have been a brave and hardy woman, and certainly deserves a monument of some kind in memory of her achievement, although it falls to the lot of few persons to have their deeds celebrated by a towering mountain for a memorial. While not as high by at least a thousand feet as Gray's Peak, it was fully as difficult of access. A high ridge of snow, which we surmounted with not a little pride and exhilaration, lay on its eastern acclivity within a few feet of the crest, a white crystalline bank gleaming in the sun. The winds hurtling over the summit were as cold and fierce as old Boreas himself, so that I was glad to wear woolen gloves and button my coat-collar close around my neck; yet it was the Fourth of July, when the people of the East were sweltering in the intense heat of their low altitudes. It was a surprise to us to find the wind so much colder here than it had been on the twenty-eighth of June on the summit of Gray's Peak, which is considerably farther north. However, there may be times when the meteorological conditions of the two peaks are reversed, blowing a gale on Gray's and whispering a zephyr on Tillie Ann.

The usual succession of birds was seen as we toiled up the slopes and steep inclines, some stopping at the timber-line and others extending their range far up toward the alpine zone. In the pine belt below the timber-line a pair of solitaires were observed flitting about on the ground and the lower branches of the trees, but vouchsafing no song. In the same woodland the mountain jays held carnival--a bacchanalian revel, judging from the noise they made; the ruby-crowned kinglets piped their galloping roundels; a number of wood-pewees--western species--were screeching, thinking themselves musical; siskins were flitting about, though not as numerous as they had been in the piny regions below Gray's Peak; and here for the first time I saw olive-sided flycatchers among the mountains. I find by consulting Professor Cooke that their breeding range is from seven thousand to twelve thousand feet. A few juncos and ruby-crowned kinglets were seen above the timber-line, while many white-crowned sparrows, some of them singing blithely, climbed as far up the mountain side as the stunted copses extended.

Oddly enough, no leucostictes were seen on this peak. Why they should make their homes on Pike's and Gray's Peaks and neglect Tillie Ann is another of those puzzles in featherdom that cannot be solved. Must a peak be over fourteen thousand feet above sea-level to meet their physiological wants in the summery season? Who can tell? There were pipits on this range, but, for some reason that was doubtless satisfactory to themselves, they were much shyer than their brothers and sisters had been on Gray's Peak and Mount Kelso; more than that, they were seen only on the slopes of the range, none of them being observed on the crest itself, perhaps on account of the cold, strong gale that was blowing across the snowy heights. A nighthawk was sailing in its erratic course over the peaks--a bit of information worth noting, none of these birds having been seen on any of the summits fourteen thousand feet high. These matters are perhaps not of supreme interest, yet they have their value as studies in comparative ornithology and are helpful in determining the locale of the several species named. In the same interest I desire to add that mountain chickadees, hermit thrushes, warbling vireos, and red-shafted flickers belong to my Breckenridge list. Besides, what I think must have been a Mexican crossbill was seen one morning among the pines, and also a large hawk and two kinds of woodpeckers, none of which tarried long enough to permit me to make sure of their identity. The crossbill-- if the individual seen was a bird of that species--wore a reddish jacket, explored the pine cones, and sang a very respectable song somewhat on the grosbeak order, quite blithe, loud, and cheerful.

On our return trip to Denver we stopped for a couple of days at the quiet village of Jefferson in South Park, and we shall never cease to be thankful that our good fairies led us to do so. What birds, think you, find residence in a green, well-watered park over nine thousand feet above sea-level, hemmed in by towering, snow-clad mountains? Spread out around you like a cyclorama lies the plateau as you descend the mountain side from Kenosha Pass; or wheel around a lofty spur of Mount Boreas, and you almost feel as if you must be entering Paradise. It was the fifth of July, and the park had donned its holiday attire, the meadows wearing robes of emerald, dappled here and there with garden spots of variegated flowers that brought more than one exclamation of delight from our lips.

SOUTH PARK FROM KENOSHA HILL

A paradise of green engirdled by snow-mantled mountains, making a summer home for western meadow-larks, Brewer's blackbirds, desert horned larks, and western Savanna sparrows.

Before leaving the village, our attention was called to a colony of cliff-swallows, the first we had seen in our touring among the mountains. Against the bare wall beneath the eaves of a barn they had plastered their adobe, bottle-shaped domiciles, hundreds of them, some in orderly rows, others in promiscuous clusters. At dusk, when we returned to the village, the birds were going to bed, and it was interesting to watch their method of retiring. The young were already grown, and the entire colony were converting their nests into sleeping berths, every one of them occupied, some of the partly demolished ones by two and three birds. But there were not enough couches to go round, and several of the birds were crowded out, and were clinging to the side of the wall on some of the protuberances left from their broken-down clay huts. It was a query in my mind whether they could sleep comfortably in that strained position, but I left them to settle that matter for themselves and in their own way.

Leaving the town, we soon found that the irrigated meadows and bush-fringed banks of the stream made habitats precisely to the taste of Brewer's blackbirds, which were quite plentiful in the park. My companion was "in clover," for numerous butterflies went undulating over the meadows, leading him many a headlong chase, but frequently getting themselves captured in his net. Thus occupied, he left me to attend to the birds. At the border of the village a little bird that was new to me flitted into view and permitted me to identify it with my glass. The little stranger was the western savanna sparrow. South Park was the only place in my Colorado rambles where I found this species, and even his eastern representative is known to me very imperfectly and only as a migrant. The park was fairly alive with savannas, especially in the irrigated portions. I wonder how many millions of them dwelt in this vast Eden of green almost twice as large as the State of Connecticut! The little cocks were incessant singers, their favorite perches being the wire fences, or weeds and grass tufts in the pastures. Their voices are weak, but very sweet, and almost as fine as the sibilant buzz of certain kinds of insects. The pretty song opens with two or three somewhat prolonged syllables, running quite high, followed by a trill much lower in the scale, and closes with a very fine, double-toned strain, delivered with the rising inflection and a kind of twist or jerk--"as if," say my notes, "the little lyrist were trying to tie a knot in his aria before letting it go." More will be said about these charming birds before the end of this chapter.

The western meadow-larks were abundant in the park, delivering with great gusto their queer, percussive chants, which, according to my notes, "so often sound as if the birds were trying to crack the whip." The park was the only place above the plains and mesas where I found these gifted fluters, with the exception of the park about Buena Vista. It would appear that the narrow mountain valleys, green and grassy though they are, do not appeal to the larks for summer homes; no, they seem to crave "ampler realms and spaces" in which to spread their wings and chant their dithyrambs.

Where the natural streams and irrigating ditches do not reach the soil of the park it is as dry and parched as the plains and mesas. In fact, the park is only a smaller and higher edition of the plains, the character of the soil and the topography of the land in both regions being identical. Never in the wet, fresh meadows, whether of plain or park, only on the arid slopes and hillocks, will you find the desert horned larks, which are certainly true to their literary cognomen, if ever birds were. How they revel in the desert! How scrupulously they draw the line on the moist and emerald areas! Surely there are "many birds of many kinds," and one might appropriately add, "of many minds," as well; for, while the blackbirds and savanna sparrows eschew the desert, the horned larks show the same dislike for the meadow. In shallow pits dug by themselves amid the sparse buffalo grass, the larks set their nests. The young had already left their nurseries at the time of my visit to the park, but were still receiving their rations from the beaks of their elders. On a level spot an adult male with an uncommonly strong voice for this species was hopping about on the ground and reciting his canticles. Seeing I was a stranger and evidently interested in all sorts of avian exploits, he decided to give an exhibition of what might be called sky-soloing, as well as dirigible ballooning. Starting up obliquely from the ground, he continued to ascend in a series of upward leaps, making a kind of aerial stairway, up, up, on and up, until he was about the size of a humming-bird framed against the blue dome of the sky. So far did he plunge into the cerulean depths that I could just discern the movement of his wings. While scaling the air he did not sing, but having reached the proper altitude, he opened his mandibles and let his ditty filtrate through the ether like a shower of spray. It could be heard quite plainly, although at best the lark's song is a weak, indefinite twitter, its peculiar characteristic being its carrying quality, which is indeed remarkable.

The soloist circled around and around in the upper air so long that I grew dizzy watching him, and my eyes became blinded by the sun and the glittering sky. How long he kept up his aerial evolutions, singing all the while, I am unprepared to announce, for I was too much engrossed in watching him to consult my timepiece; but the performance lasted so long that I was finally obliged to throw myself on my back on the ground to relieve the strain upon me, so that I might continue to follow his movements. I venture the conjecture that the show lasted from fifteen to twenty minutes; at least, it seemed that long to me in my tense state of body and mind. Finally he shot down like an arrow, making my head fairly whirl, and landed lightly on the ground, where he skipped about and resumed his roundelay as if he had not performed an extraordinary feat. This was certainly skylarking in a most literal sense. With the exception of a similar exhibition by Townsend's solitaire--to be described in the closing chapter--up in the neighborhood of Gray's Peak, it was the most wonderful avian aeronautic exploit, accompanied with song, of which I have ever been witness. It is odd, too, that a bird which is so much of a groundling--I use the term in a good sense, of course--should also be so expert a sky-scraper. I had listened to the sky song of the desert horned lark out on the plain, but there he did not hover long in the air.

The killdeer plovers are as noisy in the park as they are in an eastern pasture-field, and almost as plentiful. In the evening near the village a pair of western robins and a thieving magpie had a hard tussle along the fence of the road. The freebooter was carrying something in his beak which looked sadly like a callow nestling. He tried to hide in the fence-corners, to give himself a chance to eat his morsel, but they were hot on his trail, and at length he flew off toward the distant ridge. Where did the robins build their nests? I saw no trees in the neighborhood, but no doubt they built their adobe huts on a fence-rail or in a nook about an old building. Not a Say's phoebe had we thus far seen on this jaunt to the mountains, but here was a family near the village, and, sure enough, they were whistling their likely tunes, the first time I had ever heard them. While I had met with these birds at Glenwood and in the valley below Leadville, they had not vouchsafed a song. What is the tune they whistle? Why, to be sure, it is, "Phe-be-e! phe-be-e! phe-e-e-bie!" Their voices are stronger and more mellifluent than the eastern phoebe's, but the manner of delivery is not so sprightly and gladsome. Indeed, if I mistake not, there is a pensive strain in the lay of the western bird.

A few cowbirds, red-winged blackbirds, and spotted sandpipers were seen in the park, but they are too familiar to merit more than casual mention. However, let us return to Brewer's blackbirds. Closely as they resemble the bronzed grackles of the East, there are some marked differences between the eastern and western birds; the westerners are not so large, and their manners and nesting habits are more like those of the red-wings than the grackles. Brewer's blackbirds hover overhead as you come into the neighborhood of their nests or young, and the males utter their caveats in short squeals or screeches and the females in harsh "chacks."

The nests are set in low bushes and even on the ground, while those of the grackles are built in trees and sometimes in cavities. To be exact and scientific, Brewer's blackbirds belong to the genus Icolecophagus, and the grackles to the genus Quiscalus. In the breeding season the western birds remain in the park. That critical period over, in August and September large flocks of them, including young and old, ascend to favorite feeding haunts far above the timber-line, ranging over the slopes of the snowy mountains engirdling their summer home. Then they are in the heyday of blackbird life. Silverspot himself, made famous by

Ernest Thompson Seton, did not lead a more romantic and adventurous life, and I hope some day Brewer's blackbird will be honored by a no less effective biography.

What a to-do they make when you approach their outdoor hatchery! Yet they are sly and diplomatic. One day I tried my best to find a nest with eggs or bantlings in it, but failed, although, as a slight compensation, I succeeded in discovering three nests from which the young had flown. The old birds of both sexes circled overhead, called and pleaded and scolded, and sometimes swooped down quite close to my scalp, always veering off in time to avoid actual collision. A pair of them held choice morsels--choice for Brewer's blackbirds--in their bills, and I sat down on a tuft of sod and watched them for a couple of hours, hoping they would feed their young in plain sight and divulge their secret to me; but the sable strategists flitted here and there, hovered in the air, dropped to the ground, visiting every bush and grass-tuft but the right one, and finally the worms held in their bills disappeared, whether into their own gullets or those of their fledgelings, I could not tell. If the latter, the rascals were unconscionably wary, for my eyes were bent on them every moment--at least, I thought so. Again and again they flew off some distance, never more than a stone's throw, strutted about for a few minutes among the tufts of grass and sod, then came back with loud objurgations to the place where I sat. They seemed to be aware of my inspection the moment my field-glass was turned upon them, for they would at once cease their pretended search for insects in the grass and fly toward me with a clamorous berating giving me a big piece of their mind. At length my patience was worn out; I began to hunt for nests, and found the three empty abodes to which allusion has been made.

For the most part the female cried, "Chack! chack!" but occasionally she tried to screech like her ebon consort, her voice breaking ludicrously in the unfeminine effort. The evening before,

I had flushed a youngster about which a great hubbub was being made, but on the day of my long vigil in the meadow, I could not, by the most careful search, find a single bantling, either in or out of a nest. It is odd how effectually the young are able to conceal themselves in the short grass and straggling bushes.

Not a little attention was given to the western savanna sparrows, whose songs have already been described. Abundant proof was furnished that the breeding season for these little birds was at its height, and I determined to find a nest, if within the range of possibility. An entire forenoon was spent in discovering three nests. As you approach their domiciles, the cocks, which are always on the alert, evidently give the alarm to their sitting mates, which thereupon slip surreptitiously from the nest; and in that case how are you going to ferret out their domestic secrets?

A female--I could distinguish her from her consort by her conduct--was sitting on the post of a wire fence, preening her feathers, which was sufficient evidence that she had just come from brooding her eggs. To watch her until she went back to her nest, then make a bee-line for it--that was the plan I resolved to pursue. It is an expedient that succeeds with many birds, if the observer is very quiet and tactful. For a long time I stood in the blazing sun with my eyes bent on the little impostor. Back and forth, hither and yon, she flew, now descending to the ground and creeping slyly about in the grass, manifestly to induce me to examine the spot; then back to the fence again, chirping excitedly; then down at another place, employing every artifice to make me think the nest was where it was not; but I steadfastly refused to budge from my tracks as long as she came up in a few moments after descending, for in that case I knew that she was simply resorting to a ruse to lead me astray. Finally she went down at a point which she had previously avoided, and, as it was evident she was becoming exceedingly anxious to go back upon her eggs, I watched her like a tiger intent on his prey. Slyly she crept about in the grass, presently her chirping ceased, and she disappeared.

Several minutes passed, and she did not come up, so I felt sure she had gone down for good this time, and was sitting on her nest. Her husband exerted himself to his utmost to beguile my attention with his choicest arias, but no amount of finesse would now turn me from my purpose. I made a bee-line for the spot where I had last seen the madame, stopping not, nor veering aside for water, mud, bushes, or any other obstacle. A search of a couple of minutes brought no find, for she had employed all the strategy of which she was mistress in going to the nest, having moused along in the grass for some distance after I had last seen her. I made my search in an ever-widening circle, and at length espied some dry grass spears in a tuft right at my feet; then the little prospective mother flitted from her nest and went trailing on the ground, feigning to be fatally wounded.

Acquainted with such tactics, I did not follow her, not even with my eye, but looked down at my feet. Ah! the water sprites had been kind, for there was the dainty crib, set on a high tuft of sod raised by the winter's frosts, a little island castle in the wet marsh, cosey and dry. It was my first savanna sparrow's nest, whether eastern or western. The miniature cottage was placed under a fragment of dried cattle excrement, which made a slant roof over it, protecting it from the hot rays of the sun. Sunken slightly into the ground, the nest's rim was flush with the short grass, while the longer stems rose about it in a green, filmy wall or stockade. The holdings of the pretty cup were four pearls of eggs, the ground color white, the smaller end and middle peppered finely with brown, the larger almost solidly washed with pigment of the same tint.

Two more savannas' nests were found not long afterwards, one of them by watching the female until she settled, the other by accidentally flushing her as I walked across the marshy pasture; but neither of them was placed under a roof as the first one had been, the blue dome being their only shelter. These birdlets seem to be especially fond of soggy places in pastures, setting their nests on the little sod towers that rise above the surrounding water.

All the birds seen in the park have now been mentioned. It was an idyllic spot, and I have often regretted that I did not spend a week in rambling over it and making excursions to the engirdling ridges and peaks. A few suggestive questions arise relative to the migratory habits of the feathered tenants of a mountain park like this, for most of those that have been named are only summer residents. How do they reach this immured Eden at the time of the spring migration? One may conjecture and speculate, but one cannot be absolutely sure of the precise course of their annual pilgrimage to their summer Mecca. Of course, they come up from the plains, where the spring arrives much earlier than it does in the higher altitudes. Our nomads may ascend by easy stages along the few canyons and valleys leading up from the plains to this mountain-girt plateau; or else, rising high in air at eventide--for most birds perform their migrations at night--they may fly over the passes and mountain tops, and at dawn descend to the park.

Neither of these hypotheses is free from objection, for, on the one hand, it is not likely that birds, which cannot see in the dark, would take the risk of dashing their brains out against the cliffs and crags of the canyons by following them at night; yet they may depart from their usual habit of nocturnal migration, and make the journey up the gorges and vales by day. On the other hand, the nights are so cold in the elevated regions that the little travellers' lives might be jeopardized by nocturnal flight over the passes and peaks. There is one thing certain about the whole question, perplexing as it may be--the feathered pilgrims reach their summer quarters in some way, and seem to be very happy while they remain.

We stopped at a number of places in our run down South Platte Canyon, adding no new birds to our list, but making some interesting observations. At Cassel's a house-wren had built a nest on the veranda of the hotel where people were sitting or passing most of the time, and was feeding her tiny brood. In the copse of the hollow below the resort, the mountain song-sparrows were trilling sweetly--the only ones we had encountered in our wanderings since leaving Arvada on the plains. These musicians seem to be rather finical in their choice of summer resorts. Chaseville is about a mile below Cassel's, and was made memorable to us by the discovery of our second green-tailed towhee's nest, a description of which I have decided to reserve for the last chapter of this volume. Lincoln's sparrows descanted in rich tones at various places in the bushy vales, but were always as wild as deer, scuttling into the thickets before a fair view of them could be obtained.

The veranda of a boarding-house at Shawnee was the site of another house-wren's nest. While I stood quite close watching the little mother, she fed her bantlings twice without a quaver of fear, the youngsters chirping loudly for more of "that good dinner." At this place barn swallows were describing graceful circles and loops in the air, and a sheeny violet-green swallow squatted on the dusty road and took a sun-bath, which she did by fluffing up all her plumes and spreading out her wings and tail, so that the rays could reach every feather with their grateful warmth and light. It was a pretty performance.

A stop-over at Bailey's proved satisfactory for several reasons, among which was the finding of the Louisiana tanagers, which were the first we had seen on this trip, although many of them had been observed in the latitude of Colorado Springs. Afterwards we found them abundant in the neighborhood of Boulder. The only pigmy nuthatches of this visit were seen in a ravine above Bailey's. In the same wooded hollow I took occasion to make some special notes on the quaint calls of the long-crested jays, a task that I had thus far deferred from time to time. There was an entire family of jays in the ravine, the elders feeding their strapping youngsters in the customary manner. These birds frequently give voice to a strident call that is hard to distinguish from the cries of their kinsmen, the mountain jays. When I pursued the couple that were attending to the gastronomical wants of their children, one of the adults played a yodel on his trombone sounding like this: "Ka-ka-ka, k-wilt, k-wilt, k-wilt", the first three short syllables enunciated rapidly, and the "k-wilts" in a more measured way, with a peculiar guttural intonation, giving the full sound to the k and w. The birds became very shy when they thought themselves shadowed, not understanding what my pursuit might imply, and they gave utterance to harsh cries of warning that were different from any that had preceded. It was presently followed by a soft and friendly chatter, as if the birds were having an interview that was exclusively inter se. Then one of them startled me by breaking out in a loud, high key, crying, "Quick! quick! quick!" as fast as he could fling the syllables from his tongue. This, being translated into our human vernacular, obviously meant, "Hurry off! danger! danger!" A few minutes of silence followed the outburst, while the birds ambled farther away, and then the echoes were roused by a most raucous call, "Go-ware! go-ware! go-ware!" in a voice that would have been enough to strike terror to the heart of one who was not used to uncanny sounds in solitary places. After that outburst the family flew off, and I could hear them talking the matter over among themselves far up the mountain side, no doubt congratulating one another on their hair-breadth escape. The youngsters looked quite stylish with their quaint little blue caps and neatly fitting knickerbockers.

At Bailey's I found my first and only white-crowned sparrow's nest for this trip, although two years before I was fortunate enough to discover several nests in the valleys creeping from the foot of Pike's Peak. At dusk one evening I was walking along the railway below the village, listening to the sweetly pensive trills of the white-crowns in the bushes bordering the creek, when there was a sharp chirp in the willows, and a female white-crown darted over to my side of the stream and slipped quietly into a thick bush on the bank. I stepped down to the spot, and the pretty madame leaped away, uncovering a well-woven nest containing four white eggs speckled with dark brown. All the while her spouse was trilling with might and main on the other side of the creek, to make believe that there was nothing serious happening, no nest that any one cared anything about. His mate could not disguise her agitation by assuming nonchalance, but flitted about in the willows and chirped pitifully. I hurried away to relieve her distress. The cottages on the slopes were gay with tourists enjoying their summer outing, and beautiful Kiowa Lodge, perched on a shoulder of the mountain among embowering pines, glowed with incandescent lights, while its blithe-hearted guests pursued their chosen kinds of pastime; but none of them, I venture to assert, were happier than the little white-crown in her grassy lodge on the bank of the murmuring stream.

On the way down the canyon, as we were going to Denver, I was able to add three belted kingfishers to my bird-roll of Colorado species, the only ones I saw in the Rockies.

Our jaunt of 1901 included a trip to Boulder and a thrilling swing around the far-famed "Switzerland Trail" to Ward, perched on the mountain sides among the clouds hard by the timber-line. Almost everywhere we met with feathered comrades; in some places, especially about Boulder, many of them; but no new species were seen, and no habits observed that have not been sufficiently delineated in other parts of this book. If one could only observe all the birds all the time in all places, what a happy life the bird-lover would live! It is with feelings of mingled joy and sadness that one cons Longfellow's melodious lines:--

"Think every morning when the sun peeps through The dim, leaf-latticed windows of the grove, How jubilant the happy birds renew Their old, melodious madrigals of love! And when you think of this, remember too 'Tis always morning somewhere, and above The awakened continents, from shore to shore, Somewhere the birds are singing evermore."

A NOTABLE QUARTETTE[12]

On the plains of Colorado there dwells a feathered choralist that deserves a place in American bird literature, and the day will perhaps come when his merits will have due recognition, and then he shall have not only a monograph, but also an ode all to himself.

[12] The author is under special obligation to Mr. John P. Haines, editor of "Our Animal Friends," and president of the American Society for the Prevention of Cruelty to Animals, for publishing the contents of this chapter in his magazine in time to be included in this volume. Also for copyright privileges in connection with this and other chapters.

The bird to which I refer is called the lark bunting in plain English, or, in scientific terms, Calamospiza melanocorys. The male is a trig and handsome fellow, giving you the impression of a well-dressed gentleman in his Sunday suit of black, "with more or less of a slaty cast," as Ridgway puts it, the middle and greater wing-coverts bearing a conspicuous white patch which is both a diagnostic marking and a real ornament. In flight this patch imparts to the wing a filmy, almost semi-transparent, aspect. The bunting is about the size of the eastern bobolink, and bears some resemblance to that bird; but bobolink he is not, although sometimes mistaken for one, and even called by that name in Colorado. The fact is, those wise men, the systematists, have decided that the bobolink belongs to the family Icterid? which includes, among others, the blackbirds and orioles, while the lark bunting occupies a genus all by himself in the family Fringillid?-that is, the family of finches, sparrows, grosbeaks, and towhees. Therefore, the two birds can scarcely be called second cousins. The bunting has no white or buff on his upper parts.

Sitting on a sunny slope one June evening, I surrendered myself to the spell of the bunting, and endeavored to make an analysis of his minstrelsy. First, it must be said that he is as fond as the bobolink of rehearsing his arias on the wing, and that is, perhaps, the chief reason for his having been mistaken for that bird by careless observers. Probably the major part of his solos are recited in flight, although he can sit quietly on a weed-stalk or a fence-post and sing as sweetly, if not as ecstatically, as if he were curveting in the air. During this aerial performance he hovers gracefully, bending his wings downward, after the bobolink's manner, as if he were caressing the earth beneath him. However, a striking difference between his intermittent song-flights and those of the bobolink is to be noted. The latter usually rises in the air, soars around in a curve, and returns to the perch from which he started, or to one near by, describing something of an ellipse. The lark bunting generally rises obliquely to a certain point, then descends at about the same angle to another perch opposite the starting-point, describing what might be called the upper sides of an isosceles triangle, the base being a line near the ground, connecting the perch from which he rose and the one on which he alighted. I do not mean to say that our bunting never circles, but simply that such is not his ordinary habit, while sweeping in a circle or ellipse is the favorite pastime of the eastern bobolink. The ascent of neither bird is very high. They are far from deserving the name of skylarks.

We must give a detailed account of the bunting's song. Whatever others may think of him, I have come under the spell of his lyrical genius. True, his voice has not the loud, metallic ring, nor his chanson the medley-like, happy-go-lucky execution, that marks the musical performances of the bobolink; but his song is more mellow, rhythmic, theme-like; for he has a distinct tune to sing, and sing it he will. In fine, his song is of a different order from that of the bobolink, and, therefore, the comparison need be carried no further.

As one of these minstrels sat on a flowering weed and gave himself up to a lyrical transport, I made careful notes, and now give the substance of my elaborate entries. The song, which is intermittent, opens with three prolonged notes running high in the scale, and is succeeded by a quaint, rattling trill of an indescribable character, not without musical effect, which is followed by three double-toned long notes quite different from the opening phrases; then the whole performance is closed by an exceedingly high and fine run like an insect's hum--so fine, indeed, that the auditor must be near at hand to notice it at all. Sometimes the latter half of the score, including the second triad of long notes, is repeated before the soloist stops to take breath. It will be seen that the regular song consists of four distinct phrases, two triads and two trills. About one-third of the songs are opened in a little lower key than the rest, the remainder being correspondingly mellowed. The opening syllables, and, indeed, some other parts of the melody as well, are very like certain strains of the song-sparrow, both in execution and in quality of tone; and thus even the experienced ornithologist may sometimes be led astray. When the bunting sails into the air, he rehearses the song just described, only he is very likely to prolong it by repeating the various parts, though I think he seldom, if ever, throws them together in a hodge-podge. He seems to follow a system in his recitals, varied as many of them are. As to his voice, it is of superb timbre.

Another characteristic noted was that the buntings do not throw back their heads while singing, after the manner of the sparrows, but stretch their necks forward, and at no time do they open their mouths widely. As a rule, or at least very often, when flying, they do not begin their songs until they have almost reached the apex of their triangle; then the song begins, and it continues over the angle and down the incline until another perch is settled upon. What Lowell says of "bobolinkum" is just as true of bunting--"He runs down, a brook o' laughter, thru the air." As the sun went down behind the snow-clad mountains, a half dozen or more of the buntings rolled up the full tide of song, and I left them to their vespers and trudged back to the village, satisfied with the acquirements of this red-letter day in my ornithological journey.

However, one afternoon's study of such charming birds was not enough to satisfy my curiosity, for no females had been seen and no nests discovered. About ten days later, more attention was given them. In a meadow not far from the hamlet of Arvada, between Denver and the mountains, I found a colony of buntings one morning, swinging in the air and furnishing their full quota of the matutinal concert, in which many other birds had a leading part, among them being western meadow-larks, western robins, Bullock's orioles, American and Arkansas goldfinches, mountain song-sparrows, lazuli finches, spurred towhees, black-headed grosbeaks, summer warblers, western Maryland yellow-throats, and Townsend's solitaires. It has seldom been my fortune to listen to a finer pot-pourri of avian music.

At first only male buntings were seen. Surely, I thought, there must be females in the neighborhood, for when male birds are singing so lustily about a place, their spouses are usually sitting quietly on nests somewhere in bush or tree or grass. I hunted long for a nest, trudging about over the meadow, examining many a grass-tuft and weed-clump, hoping to flush a female and discover her secret; but my quest was vain. It is strange how difficult it is to find nests in Colorado, either on the plains or in the mountains. The birds seem to be adepts in the fine arts of concealment and secret-keeping. Presently several females were seen flying off over the fields and returning, obviously to feed their young. There was now some colorable prospect of finding a nest. A mother bird appeared with a worm in her bill, and you may rely upon it I did not permit her to slip from my sight until I saw her drop to the ground, hop about stealthily for a few moments, then disappear, and presently fly up minus the worm. Scarcely daring to breathe, I followed a direct course to the weed-clump from which she had risen. And there was a nest, sure enough--my first lark bunting's-- set in a shallow pit of the ground, prettily concealed and partly roofed over by the flat and spreading weed-stalk. Four half-fledged youngsters lay panting in the little cradle, the day being very warm. I lifted one of them from the nest, and held it in my hand for a minute or two, and even touched it with my lips, my first view of lark-bunting babies being something of an event--I had almost said an epoch--in my experience. Replacing the youngster in its crib, I stepped back a short distance and watched the mother bird returning with another mouthful of "goodies," and feeding her bantlings four. She was not very shy, and simply uttered a fine chirp when I went too close to her nestlings, while her gallant consort did not even chirp, but tried to divert my attention by repeatedly curveting in the air and singing his choicest measures. This was the only bunting's nest I found, although I made long and diligent search for others, as you may well believe when I state that a half day was spent in gathering the facts recorded in the last two paragraphs.

In the afternoon I watched a female in another field for a long time, but she was too wary to betray her secret. In this case the male, instead of beguiling me with song, flitted about and mingled his fine chirps with those of his anxious mate. On my way across the plains, some two weeks later, I discovered that the lark buntings do not dwell only in well-watered meadows, but also in the most arid localities. Still, I am inclined to think they do not build their nests far from refreshing streams. When the breeding season is over, they range far and wide over the plains in search of insects that are to their taste. From the car window many of them were observed all along the way to a distance of over sixty miles east of Denver. At that time the males, females, and young were moving from place to place, mostly in scattering flocks, the breeding season being past. A problem that puzzled me a little was where they obtain water for drinking and bathing purposes, but no doubt such blithe and active birds are able to "look out for number one."

The second member of our lyrical quartette is the elegant green-tailed towhee, known scientifically as Pipilo chlorurus. The pretty green-tails are quite wary about divulging their domestic secrets, and for a time I was almost in despair of finding even one of their nests. In vain I explored with exhausting toil many a steep mountain side, examining every bush and beating every copse within a radius of many rods.

My purpose was to flush the female from her nest, a plan that succeeds with many birds; but in this instance I was disappointed. It is possible that, when an intruder appears in their nesting haunts, the males, which are ever on the lookout, call their spouses from the nests, and then "snap their fingers," so to speak, at the puzzled searcher.

However, by watching the mother birds carrying worms in their bills I succeeded in finding two nests. The first was at Breckenridge, and, curiously enough, in a vacant lot at the border of the town, not on a steep slope, but on a level spot near the bank of Blue River. The mother bird had slyly crept to her nest while I watched, and remained firmly seated until I bent directly over her, when she fluttered away, trailing a few feet to draw my attention to herself. It was a cosey nest site--in a low, thick bush, beneath a rusty but well-preserved piece of sheet-iron which made a slant roof over the cradle. It contained three callow bantlings, which innocently opened their carmine-lined mouths when I stirred the leaves above them. It seemed to be an odd location for the nest of a bird that had always appeared so wild and shy. The altitude of the place is nine thousand five hundred and twenty feet.

My second green-tail's nest was in South Platte Canyon, near a station called Chaseville, its elevation being about eight thousand five hundred feet. I was walking along the dusty wagon road winding about the base of the mountain, when a little bird with a worm in her bill flitted up the steep bank a short distance and disappeared among the bushes. The tidbit in her bill gave me a clew to the situation; so I scrambled up the steep place, and presently espied a nest in a bush, about a foot and a half from the ground. As had been anticipated, it turned out to be a green-tailed towhee's domicile, as was proved by the presence and uneasy chirping of a pair of those birds. While the nest at Breckenridge was set on the ground, this one was placed on the twigs of thick bushes, showing that these birds, like their eastern relatives, are fond of diversity in selecting nesting places.

This nest contained four bantlings, already well fledged. My notes say that their mouths were yellow-lined, and that the fleshy growths at the corners of their bills were yellow. Does the lining of the juvenile green-tail's mouth change from red to yellow as he advances in age? My notes certainly declare that the nestlings at Breckenridge had carmine-lined mouths. For the present I cannot settle the question either affirmatively or negatively.

Here I perpetrated a trick which I have ever since regretted. The temptation to hold a baby green-tail in my hand and examine it closely was so strong that, as carefully as I could, I drew one from its grassy crib and held it in my palm, noting the green tinting already beginning to show on its wings and back. Its tail was still too stubby to display the ornamentation that gives the species its popular name. So much was learned, but at the expense of the little family's peace of mind. As I held the bantling in my hand, the frightened mamma uttered a series of pitiful calls that were new to my ears, consisting of two notes in a low, complaining tone; it was more of an entreaty than a protest. Afterwards I heard the green-tails also give voice to a fine chirp almost like that of a chipping sparrow.

The mother's call seemed to strike terror to the hearts of her infant brood, for, as I attempted to put the baby back into its crib, all four youngsters set up a loud to-do, and sprang, panic stricken, over the rim, tumbling, fluttering, and falling through the network of twigs to the ground, a couple of them rolling a few feet down the dusty bank. Again and again I caught them and put them back into the nest, but they would not remain there, so I was compelled to leave them scrambling about among the bushes and rocks. I felt like a buccaneer, a veritable Captain Kidd. My sincere hope is that none of the birdkins came to grief on account of their premature flight from the nest. The next morning old and young were chirping about the place as I passed, and I hurried away, feeling sad that science and sentiment must sometimes come into conflict.

One day in the latter part of June, as I was climbing the steep side of a mesa in the neighborhood of Golden, my ear was greeted by a new style of bird music, which came lilting sweetly down to me from the height. It had a kind of wild, challenging ring about it, as if the singer were daring me to venture upon his demesne at my peril. A hard climb brought me at length within range of the little performer, who was blowing his Huon's horn from the pointed top of a large stone on the mesa's side. My field-glass was soon fixed upon him, revealing a little bird with a long beak, decurved at the end, a grayish-brown coat quite thickly barred and mottled on the wings and tail, and a vest of warm white finely sprinkled with a dusky gray. A queer, shy, timid little thing he was. Afterwards I met him often, but never succeeded in gaining his confidence or winning a single concession from him. He was the rock wren (Salpinctes obsoletus)--a species that is unknown east of the Great Plains, one well deserving a place in literature.

I was especially impressed with his peculiar style of minstrelsy, so different from anything I had ever heard in the bird realm. While the song was characterized by much variety, it usually opened with two or three loud, clear syllables, somewhat prolonged, sounding, as has been said, like a challenge, followed by a peculiar bubbling trill that seemed fairly to roll from the piper's tongue. Early one morning a few days later I heard a brilliant vocalist descanting from the top of a pump in a wide field among the foothills. How wildly his tones rang out on the crisp morning air! I seemed to be suddenly transported to another part of the world, his style of music was so new, so foreign to my ear. My pencilled notes say of this particular minstrel: "Very musical--great variety of notes--clear, loud, ringing--several runs slightly like Carolina's--others suggest Bewick's--but most of them sui generis."

Let us return to the first rock wren I saw. He was exceedingly shy, scurrying off to a more distant perch--another stone--as I approached. Sometimes he would run down among the bushes and rocks like a mouse, then glide to the top of another stone, and fling his pert little aria at the intruder. It was interesting to note that he most frequently selected for a singing perch the top of a high, pointed rock where he could command a view of his surroundings and pipe a note of warning to his mate at the approach of a supposed enemy. Almost every conspicuous rock on the acclivity bore evidence of having been used as a lookout by the little sentinel.

This wren is well named, for his home is among the rocks, in the crannies and niches of which his mate hides her nest so effectually that you must look long for it, and even after the most painstaking search you may not be able to find it. The little husband helps to lead you astray. He will leap upon a rock and send forth his bell-like peal, as if he were saying, "Right here, right here, here is our nest!" but when you go to the spot, he flits off to another rock and sounds the same challenge. And so you can form no idea of the nest site. My nearest approach to finding a nest was among the rocks and cliffs on the summit of a mountain a few miles from Golden, where an adult bird was seen to feed a youngster that had already flown from the nursery. It was interesting to know that the rock wrens breed at so high an altitude. However, they are not an alpine species, none having been seen by the writer over eight thousand feet above sea-level, although they have been known to ascend to an altitude of twelve thousand feet.

The fourth member of our feathered quartette was the oddest of all. On the thirtieth of June my companion and I were riding slowly down the mountain side a few miles below Gray's Peak, which we had scaled two days before. My ear was struck by a flicker's call above us, so I dismounted from my burro, and began to clamber up the hillside. Presently I heard a song that seemed one moment to be near at hand, the next far away, now to the right, now to the left, and anon directly above me. To my ear it was a new kind of bird minstrelsy. I climbed higher and higher, and yet the song seemed to be no nearer. It had a grosbeak-like quality, I fancied, and I hoped to find either the pine or the evening grosbeak, for both of which I had been making anxious search. The shifting of the song from point to point struck me as odd, and it was very mystifying.

Higher and higher I climbed, the mountain side being so steep that my breath came in gasps, and I was often compelled to throw myself on the ground to recover strength. At length a bird darted out from the pines several hundred feet above me, rose high into the air, circled and swung this way and that for a long time, breaking at intervals into a song which sifted down to me faintly through the blue distance. How long it remained on the wing I do not know, but it was too long for my eyes to endure the strain of watching it. Through my glass a large part of the wings showed white or yellowish-white, and seemed to be almost translucent in the blaze of the sunlight. What could this wonderful haunter of the sky be? It was scarcely possible that so roly-poly a bird as a grosbeak could perform so marvelous an exploit on the wing.

I never worked harder to earn my salary than I did to climb that steep and rugged mountain side; but at last I reached and penetrated the zone of pines, and finally, in an area covered with dead timber, standing and fallen, two feathered strangers sprang in sight, now flitting among the lower branches and now sweeping to the ground. They were not grosbeaks, that was sure; their bills were quite slender, their bodies lithe and graceful, and their tails of well-proportioned length. Save in color, they presented a decidedly thrush-like appearance, and their manners were also thrush-like.

Indeed, the colors and markings puzzled me not a little. The upper parts were brownish-gray of various shades, the wings and tail for the most part dusky, the wing-coverts, tertials, and some of the quills bordered and tipped with white, also the tail. The white of both wings and tail became quite conspicuous when they were spread. This was the feathered conundrum that flitted about before me. The birds were about the size of the hermit thrushes, but lither and suppler. They ambled about gracefully, and did not seem to be very shy, and presently one of them broke into a song--the song that I had previously heard, only it was loud and ringing and well articulated, now that I was near the singer. Again and again they lifted their rich voices in song. When they wandered a little distance from each other, they called in affectionate tones, giving their "All's well."

Then one of them, no doubt the male, darted from a pine branch obliquely into the air, and mounted up and up and up, in a series of graceful leaps, until he was a mere speck against the blue dome, gyrating to and fro in zigzag lines, or wheeling in graceful circles, his song dribbling faintly down to me at frequent intervals. A thing of buoyancy and grace, more angel than bird, that wonderful winged creature floated about in the cerulean sky; how long I do not know, whether five minutes, or ten, or twenty, but so long that at last I flung myself upon my back and watched him until my eyes ached. He kept his wings in constant motion, the white portions making them appear filmy as the sun shone upon them. Suddenly he bent his head, partly folded his wings, and swept down almost vertically like an arrow, alighting safe somewhere among the pines. I have seen other birds performing aerial evolutions accompanied with song, but have never known one to continue so long on the wing.

What was this wonderful bird? It was Townsend's solitaire (Myadestes townsendii)--a bird which is peculiar to the West, especially to the Rocky Mountains, and which belongs to the same family as the thrushes and bluebirds. No literature in my possession contains any reference to this bird's astonishing aerial flight and song, and I cannot help wondering whether other bird-students have witnessed the interesting exploit.

Subsequently I found a pair of solitaires on the plains near

Arvada. The male was a powerful singer. Many of his outbursts were worthy of the mocking-bird, to some of whose runs they bore a close resemblance. He sang almost incessantly during the half day I spent in the neighborhood, my presence seeming to inspire him to the most prodigious lyrical efforts of which he was master. Sometimes he would sit on the top of a bush or a fence-post, but his favorite perches were several ridges of sand and gravel. His flight was the picture of grace, and he had a habit of lifting his wings, now one, now the other, and often both, after the manner of the mocking-bird on a chimney-top. He and his mate did not utter a chirp, but made a great to-do by singing, and finally I discovered that all the fuss was not about a nest, but about a hulking youngster that had outgrown his kilts and looked very like a brown thrasher. Neither of this second pair of solitaires performed any evolutions in the upper air; nor did another pair that I found far up a snow-clad mountain near Breckenridge, on the other side of the Continental Divide.

The scientific status of this unique bird is interesting. He is a species of the genus Myadestes, which belongs to the family Turdid? including the thrushes, stone-chats, and bluebirds, as well as the solitaires. He is therefore not a thrush, but is closely related to the genus Turdus, occupying the same relative position in the avi-faunal system. According to Doctor Coues the genus includes about twenty species, only one of which--the one just described--is native to the United States, the rest being found in the West Indies and Central and South America. Formerly the solitaires comprised a subfamily among the chatterers, but a later and more scientific classification places them in a genus under the head of Turdid?

The range of Townsend's solitaire is from the plains of Colorado to the Pacific coast and north to British Columbia. According to Robert Ridgway, he has even been met with "casually" in Illinois. In Colorado many of the solitaires are permanent residents in the mountains, remaining there throughout the winter. Some of them, however, visit the plains during the fall, winter, and spring. In the winter they may be found from the lower valleys to an elevation of ten thousand feet, while they are known to breed as high as twelve thousand feet. The nests are placed on the ground among rocks, fallen branches and logs, and are loosely constructed of sticks and grass. From three to six eggs compose a set, the ground color being white, speckled with reddish brown. Doctor Coues says the birds feed on insects and berries, and are "capable of musical expression in an exalted degree." With this verdict the writer is in full accord.

CHECK-LIST OF COLORADO BIRDS

The following list includes all the species and varieties, so far as known to naturalists, occurring in the State of Colorado. Of course, these birds as families are not restricted to that State, and therefore the catalogue comprehends many of the species to be found in adjacent and even more remote parts of the country. Aside from the author's own observations, he is indebted for a large part of the matter comprised in this list to Professor Wells W. Cooke's pamphlet, entitled, "The Birds of Colorado," with the several appendixes, and to the invaluable manuals of Mr. Ridgway and Dr. Coues.

According to the latest information accessible to the writer, 389 species and varieties occur in Colorado, of which 243 are known to breed. This is a superb record, and is excelled by only two other States in the Union, namely, Texas and California. Colorado's splendid list is to be explained on the ground of its wonderful variety of climate, altitude, soil, and topographical features, such as its plains, foothills, lower mountains, and towering peaks and ranges, bringing within its boundaries many eastern, boreal, middle western, and far western forms.

The author's preference would have been to begin the roll with the most interesting birds, those to which he gave the largest share of his attention, namely, the oscines, but he has decided to follow the order and nomenclature of the Check-List of North American birds as arranged by the American Ornithologists' Union. In deference to the general reader, however, he has placed the English name of each bird first, then the scientific designation. The numbers correspond to the American Check-List. By noting those omitted, the reader will readily discover what species have not been found in Colorado.

1. =Western grebe.= AHMOPHORUS OCCIDENTALIS. Rare migrant; western species, chiefly interior regions of North America.

2. =Holboell's grebe.= COLYMBUS HOLBOELLII. Rare migrant; breeds far north; range, all of North America.

3. =Horned grebe.= COLYMBUS AURITUS. Rare migrant; range, almost the same as the last.

4. =American eared grebe.= COLYMBUS NIGRICOLLIS CALIFORNICUS. Summer resident; rare in eastern, common in western Colorado; breeds from plains to 8,000 feet; partial to alkali lakes; western species.

6. =Pied-billed grebe.= PODILYMBUS PODICEPS. Summer resident, rare; common in migration; breeds in northern part of State; sometimes winters in southern part.

7. =Loon.= GAVIA IMBER. Migrant; occasionally winter resident; not known to breed in State.

8. =Yellow-billed loon.= GAVIA ADAMSII. Migrant; rare or

accidental.

9. =Black-throated loon.= GAVIA ARCTICA. Rare fall and winter visitant.

37. =Parasitic jaeger.= STERCORARIUS PARASITICUS. Fall and winter resident; rare.

40. =Kittiwake.= RISSA TRIDACTYLA. Rare or accidental in winter.

49. =Western gull.= LARUS OCCIDENTALIS. Pacific Coast bird; accidental in Colorado; only one record.

51a. =American herring gull.= LARUS ARGENTATUS SMITHSONIANUS. Rare migrant; range, the whole of North America.

53. =California gull.= LARUS CALIFORNICUS. Western species; breeds abundantly in Utah; only three records for Colorado.

54. =Ring-billed gull.= LARUS DELAWARENSIS. Not uncommon summer resident; common in migration; breeds as high as 7,500 feet; range, whole of North America.

58. =Laughing gull.= LARUS ATRICILLA. Bird of South Atlantic and Gulf States; once accidental in Colorado.

59. =Franklin's gull.= LARUS FRANKLINII. Rare migrant; range, interior of North America.

60. =Bonaparte's gull.= LARUS PHILADELPHIA. Rare migrant; not uncommon in a few localities; range, whole of North America.

62. =Sabine's gull.= XEMA SABINII. Rare winter visitant; breeds in the arctic regions.

69. =Forster's tern.= STERNA FORSTERI. Rare summer resident; common migrant; habitat, temperate North America.

71. =Arctic tern.= STERNA PARADIS. Very rare migrant; but two records; breeding habitat, circumpolar regions.

77. =Black tern.= HYDROCHELIDON NIGRA SURINAMENSIS. Common summer resident; both sides of range; habitat, temperate North America; in winter south as far as Brazil and Chili.

120. =Double-crested cormorant.= PHALACROCORAX DILOPHUS. Perhaps breeds in Colorado, as it breeds abundantly in Utah; all present records from eastern foothills.

125. =American white pelican.= PELECANUS ERYTHRORHYNCHOS. Once a common migrant; a few remained to breed; now rare; still noted on both sides of the range.

129. =American merganser.= MERGANSER AMERICANUS. Resident; common migrant and winter sojourner; a few breed in mountains and parks; generally distributed in North America.

130. =Red-breasted merganser.= MERGANSER SERRATOR. Rare winter sojourner; common migrant; breeds far north.

131. =Hooded merganser.= LOPHODYTES CUCULLATUS. Rare resident both summer and winter; breeds in eastern part and in the mountains; general range, North America.

132. =Mallard.= ANAS BOSCHAS. Very common in migration; common in winter; breeds below 9,000 feet, on plains as well as in mountains; general range, whole northern hemisphere.

134a. =Mottled duck.= ANAS FULVIGULA MACULOSA. Rare migrant; an eastern species, sometimes wandering west to plains.

135. =Gadwall.= CHAULELASMUS STREPERUS. Summer resident; common in migration; breeds on plains; also in sloughs and small lakes at an elevation of 11,000 feet in southern part of State; breeds abundantly at San Luis Lakes.

137. =Baldpate.= MARECA AMERICANA. Summer resident; breeds from plains to 8,000 feet.

139. =Green-winged teal.= NETTION CAROLINENSIS. Common summer resident; abundant in migration; a few breed on the plains; more in mountains and upper parks.

140. =Blue-winged teal.= QUERQUEDULA DISCORS. Same records as preceding.

141. =Cinnamon teal.= QUERQUEDULA CYANOPTERA. Common summer resident; breeds both east and west of the range; a western species; in winter south to Chili, Argentina, and Falkland Islands; sometimes strays east as far as Illinois and Louisiana.

142. =Shoveller.= SPATULA CLYPEATA. Summer resident; abundant in migration; breeds in suitable localities, but prefers mountain parks 8,000 feet in altitude; breeds throughout its range, which is the whole of North America.

143. =Pintail=. DAFILA ACUTA. Rare summer and winter resident; common migrant; mostly breeds in the North.

144. =Wood duck.= AIX SPONSA. Rare summer resident.

146. =Redhead.= AYTHYA AMERICANA. Common migrant; breeds far north; migrates early in spring.

147. =Canvas-back.= AYTHYA VALLISNERIA. Migrant; not common; breeds far north.

148. =Scaup duck.= AYTHYA MARILA. Rare migrant; both sides of the range; breeds far north.

149. =Lesser scaup duck.= AYTHYA AFFINIS. Migrant; not common; a little more common than preceding.

150. =Ring-necked duck.= AYTHYA COLLARIS. Rare migrant, though common in Kansas; breeds in far North.

151. =American golden-eye.= CLANGULA CLANGULA AMERICANA. Rare migrant; breeds far north.

152. =Barrow's golden-eye.= CLANGULA ISLANDICA. Summer and winter resident; a northern species, but breeds in mountains of Colorado, sometimes as high as 10,000 feet; rare on plains.

153. =Buffle-head.= CHARITONETTA ALBEOLA. Common migrant throughout State; breeds in the North.

154. =Old squaw.= HARELDA HYEMALIS. Rare winter visitor; a northern species.

155. =Harlequin duck.= HISTRIONICUS HISTRIONICUS. Resident; not common; a northern species, but a few breed in

mountains at an altitude of 7,000 to 10,000 feet.

160. =American eider.= SOMATERIA DRESSERI. Very rare; only two records--one somewhat uncertain.

163. =American scoter.= OIDEMIA AMERICANA. Rare winter visitor; northern bird, in winter principally along the sea-coast, but a few visit the larger inland lakes.

165. =White-winged scoter.= OIDEMIA DEGLANDI. Same habits as preceding; perhaps rarer.

166. =Surf scoter.= OIDEMIA PERSPICILLATA. Same as preceding.

167. =Ruddy duck.= ERISMATURA JAMAICENSIS. Common summer resident; both sides of the range; breeds from plains to 10,000 feet; a beautiful bird; author's observations given in Chapter VII.

169. =Lesser snow goose.= CHEN HYPERBOREA. Migrant and winter resident; not common; breeds far north.

169a. =Greater snow goose.= CHEN HYPERBOREA NIVALIS. Rare migrant; only two records; the eastern form, which does not come regularly as far west as Colorado.

171a. =American white-fronted goose.= ANSER ALBIFRONS GAMBELI. Rare migrant; breeds far northward.

172. =Canada goose.= BRANTA CANADENSIS. Summer and winter resident; rare, except locally; common in migration; breeds about secluded lakes at 10,000 feet.

172a. =Hutchins's goose.= BRANTA CANADENSIS HUTCHINSII. Common migrant; breeds in the North; a few may winter in the State.

172c. =Cackling goose.= BRANTA CANADENSIS MINIMA. One record; Pacific coast bird; breeds in Alaska.

173. =Brant.= BRANTA BERNICLA. Rare or accidental migrant; an eastern species seldom coming west; breeds only within the Arctic Circle.

180. =Whistling swan.= OLOR COLUMBIANUS. Migrant; not common; formerly fairly plentiful; breeds far northward.

181. =Trumpeter swan.= OLOR BUCCINATOR. Rare migrant; not so common as preceding; breeds from Iowa and Dakota northward.

183. =Roseate spoonbill.= AJAJA AJAJA. Accidental; two instances; habitat, tropical and subtropical America.

184. =White ibis.= GUARA ALBA. Rare migrant; one taken on plains; habitat, tropical and subtropical America, coming north as far as Great Salt Lake and South Dakota.

[185.] =Scarlet ibis.= GUARA RUBRA. Accidental; one specimen taken; a wonderful record for this tropical species.

186. =Glossy ibis.= PLEGADIS AUTUMNALIS. Accidental; two fine specimens taken in the State; this is far out of its ordinary tropical range.

187. =White-faced glossy ibis.= PLEGADIS GUARAUNA. Summer visitor; rare; fairly common in New Mexico and Arizona;

sometimes wanders into Colorado; Aiken found it breeding at San Luis Lakes.

188. =Wood ibis.= TANTALUS LOCULATOR. Rare summer visitor; southern range.

190. =American bittern.= BOTAURUS LENTIGINOSUS. Common summer resident; breeds throughout the State, from plains to about 7,000 feet.

191. =Least bittern.= ARDETTA EXILIS. Rare summer visitor; a few records east of mountains; one specimen seen west of the divide.

194. =Great blue heron.= ARDEA HERODIAS. Summer resident; common in migration; seldom goes far up in the mountains, though Mr. Aiken found one at an altitude of 9,000 feet.

196. =American egret.= ARDEA EGRETTA. Rare or accidental; one seen; general range, the whole of the United States; in winter south to Chili and Patagonia.

197. =Snowy heron.= ARDEA CANDIDISSIMA. Summer visitor; not known to breed; the highest altitude is the one taken near Leadville, 10,000 feet.

198. =Reddish egret.= ARDEA RUFESCENS. Rare or accidental; only two specimens secured; southern range.

202. =Black-crowned night heron.= NYCTICORAX NYCTICORAX N 芗 IUS. Summer resident; not common; local; more plentiful in migration.

203. =Yellow-crowned night heron.= NYCTICORAX VIOLACEUS. Rare summer visitor; southern species; not known to breed in State.

204. =Whooping crane.= GRUS AMERICANA. Rare migrant; more common east of Colorado.

205. =Little brown crane.= GRUS CANADENSIS. Migrant; few taken; northern breeder.

206. =Sandhill crane.= GRUS MEXICANA. Summer resident; not uncommon locally; in migration common; breeds as high as 8,000 feet; has been seen in autumn passing over the highest peaks.

212. =Virginia rail.= RALLUS VIRGINIANUS. Summer resident; not uncommon; breeds on plains and in mountains to at least 7,500 feet.

214. =Sora.= PORZANA CAROLINA. Common summer resident; breeds from plains to 9,000 feet.

216. =Black rail.= PORZANA JAMAICENSIS. Rare migrant; one specimen secured.

219. =Florida gallinule.= GALLINULA GALEATA. Summer visitor, not known to breed.

221. =American coot.= FULICA AMERICANA. Common summer resident; breeds on plains and in mountain parks.

222. =Red phalarope.= CRYMOPHILUS FULICARIUS. Migrant; rare; once taken at Loveland by Edw. A. Preble, July 25, 1895. Breeds far north.

223. =Northern phalarope.= PHALAROPUS LOBATUS. Migrant; not uncommon; breeds far northward.

224. =Wilson's phalarope.= STEGANOPUS TRICOLOR. Common summer resident; more common in migration; breeds below 6,000 feet.

225. =American avocet.= RECURVIROSTRA AMERICANA. Common summer resident; occurs frequently on the plains; less frequent in mountains.

226. =Black-necked stilt.= HIMANTOPUS MEXICANUS. Summer resident; most common in the mountains, going as high as 8,000 feet; more common west of range than east.

228. =American woodcock.= PHILOHELA MINOR. Rare summer resident; Colorado the extreme western limit of its range, going only to foothills.

230. =Wilson's snipe.= GALLINAGO DELICATA. Rare summer resident; common migrant; winter resident, rare; found as high as 10,000 feet.

232. =Long-billed dowitcher.= MACRORHAMPHUS SCOLOPACEUS. Somewhat common migrant; all records restricted to plains; breeds far northward.

233. =Stilt sandpiper.= MICROPALAMA HIMANTOPUS. Rare migrant; breeds north of United States.

239. =Pectoral sandpiper.= TRINGA MACULTA. Common migrant; occurs from the plains to the great height of 13,000 feet.

240. =White-rumped sandpiper.= TRINGA FUSCICOLLIS. Not

uncommon migrant; a bird of the plains, its western limit being the base of the Rockies; breeds in the far North.

241. =Baird's sandpiper.= TRINGA BAIRDII. Abundant migrant; breeds far north; returns in August and ranges over mountains sometimes at height of 13,000 to 14,000 feet, feeding on grasshoppers.

242. =Least sandpiper.= TRINGA MINUTILLA. Common migrant; found from plains to 7,000 feet.

243a. =Red-backed sandpiper.= TRINGA ALPINA PACIFICA. Rare migrant; only three records; range, throughout North America.

246. =Semipalmated sandpiper.= EREUNETES PUSILLUS. Common migrant; from the plains to 8,000 feet.

247. =Western sandpiper.= EREUNETES OCCIDENTALIS. Rare migrant; breeds in the remote North; western species, but in migration occurs regularly along the Atlantic coast.

248. =Sanderling.= CALIDRIS ARENARIA. Rare migrant, on plains; range nearly cosmopolitan; breeds only in northern part of northern hemisphere.

249. =Marbled godwit.= LIMOSA FEDOA. Migrant; not common; a bird of the plains, but seldom seen; occasionally found in the mountains.

254. =Greater yellow-legs.= TOTANUS MELANOLEUCUS. Common migrant; in favorable localities below 8,000 feet.

255. =Yellow-legs.= TOTANUS FLAVIPES. Common migrant; distribution same as preceding.

256. =Solitary sandpiper.= HELODROMAS SOLITARIUS. Summer resident; not common; in migration, common; breeds from plains to 10,000 feet.

258a. =Western willet.= SYMPHEMIA SEMIPALMATA INORNATA. Summer resident; not common; common migrant, especially in the fall; breeds from plains to 7,000 feet.

261. =Bartramian sandpiper.= BARTRAMIA LONGICAUDA. Common summer resident; abundant in migration; a bird of the plains; rare west of mountains.

263. =Spotted sandpiper.= ACTITIS MACULARIA. Abundant summer resident; breeds on the plains and at all intermediate altitudes to 12,000 feet, even on top of mountains of that height, if a lake or pond can be found; in fall, ranges above timber-line to 14,000 feet; some may remain throughout winter.

264. =Long-billed curlew.= NUMENIUS LONGIROSTRIS. Common summer resident; breeds on the plains; also in Middle and South Parks; found on both sides of the range.

265. =Hudsonian curlew.= NUMENIUS HUDSONICUS. Rare migrant; all records thus far from the plains; general range, North America.

270. =Black-bellied plover.= SQUATAROLA SQUATAROLA. Migrant, not common; bird of plains below 5,000 feet; breeds far north.

272. =American golden plover.= CHARADRIUS DOMINICUS. Migrant, not common; same record as preceding.

273. =Killdeer.= CHARADRIUS VOCIFERA. Abundant summer resident; arrives early in spring; breeds most abundantly on plains and at base of foothills, but is far from rare at an altitude of 10,000 feet.

274. =Semipalmated plover.= CHARADRIUS SEMIPALMATA. Migrant, not common; breeds near the Arctic Circle.

281. =Mountain plover.= CHARADRIUS MONTANA. Common summer resident; in spite of its name, a bird of the plains rather than the mountains; yet sometimes found in parks at an altitude of 8,000 and even 9,000 feet. Its numbers may be estimated from the fact that in one day of August a sportsman shot one hundred and twenty-six birds, though why he should indulge in such wholesale slaughter the author does not understand.

283. =Turnstone.= ARENARIA INTERPRES. Rare migrant; breeding grounds in the north; cosmopolitan in range, but chiefly along sea-coasts.

289. =Bob-white.= COLINUS VIRGINIANUS. Resident; somewhat common locally; good reason to believe that all the quails of the foothills are descendants of introduced birds, while those of the eastern border of the plains are native. A few were introduced some years ago into Estes Park, and are still occasionally noticed.

293. =Scaled partridge.= CALLIPEPLA SQUAMATA. Resident; common locally; southern species, but more common than the bob-white at Rocky Ford, Col.

294. =California partridge.= LOPHORTYX CALIFORNICUS. Resident, local; introduced at Grand Junction, Col., and have flourished so abundantly as to become troublesome to gardeners.

295. =Gambel's partridge.= LOPHORTYX GAMBELII. Resident, rare; known only in southwestern part of the State; a western species.

297. =Dusky grouse.= DENDRAGAPUS OBSCURUS. Resident; mountain dwellers; breed from 7,000 feet to timber-line; in September wander above timber-line to 12,500 feet, feeding on grasshoppers; remain in thick woods in winter.

300b. =Gray ruffed grouse.= BONASA UMBELLUS UMBELLOIDES. Rare resident; a more northern species, but a few breed in Colorado just below timber-line; winters in higher foothills.

304. =White-tailed ptarmigan.= LAGOPUS LEUCURUS. Common resident; one of the most strictly alpine species; breeds entirely above timber-line from 11,500 to 13,500 feet; thence ranging to the summits of the highest peaks. Only in severest winter weather do they come down to timber-line; rarely to 8,000 feet. In winter they are white; in summer fulvous or dull grayish-buff, barred and spotted with black. This bird is colloquially called the "mountain quail." The brown-capped leucosticte is the only other Colorado species that has so high a range.

305. =Prairie hen.= TYMPANUCHUS AMERICANUS. Resident; uncommon and local.

308b. =Prairie sharp-tailed grouse.= PEDIOECETES PHASIANELLUS CAMPESTRIS. Resident, not common; once common, but killed and driven out by pothunters; some breed in Middle Park; noted in winter at 9,500 feet.

309. =Sage grouse.= CENTROCERCUS UROPHASIANUS.

Common resident. "As its name implies, it is an inhabitant of the artemisia or sage-brush plains, and is scarcely found elsewhere." Ranges from plains to 9,500 feet.

310. =Mexican turkey.= MELEAGRIS GALLOPAVO. Rare local resident; southern part of the State.

310a. =Wild turkey.= MELEAGRIS GALLOPAVO FERA. Resident; rare; once abundant, but will probably soon be exterminated; not certain whether Colorado birds are eastern or western forms.

312. =Band-tailed pigeon.= COLUMBA FASCIATA. Summer resident; local; breeds from 5,000 to 7,000 feet and occasionally higher.

316. =Mourning dove.= ZENAIDURA MACROURA. Summer resident; very abundant; breeds everywhere below the pine region up to 10,000 feet, though usually a little lower; in fall ranges up to 12,000 feet.

319. =White-winged dove.= MELOPELIA LEUCOPTERA. Four records of this straggler in Colorado; its usual range is subtropical, though not uncommon as far north as the southern border of the United States.

325. =Turkey vulture.= CATHARTES AURA. Common summer resident; breeds from plains to 10,000 and even 12,000 feet.

327. =Swallow-tailed kite.= ELANOIDES FORFICATUS. Summer visitor; rare or accidental; bird of the plains, not regularly west of central Kansas.

329. =Mississippi kite.= ICTINIA MISSISSIPPIENSIS.

Accidental; two records; a bird of eastern and southern United States, and southward.

331. =Marsh hawk.= CIRCUS HUDSONIUS. Common resident; most common in migration; a few remain throughout winter; breeds on plains, and in mountains to 10,000 feet; in fall may be seen at 14,000 feet.

332. =Sharp-shinned hawk.= ACCIPITER VELOX. Common resident; much more common in mountains than on plains; breeds up to 10,000 feet.

333. COOPER'S HAWK. ACCIPITER COOPERI. Common resident; breeds from plains to 9,000 feet.

334. =American goshawk.= ACCIPITER ATRICAPILLUS. Resident; not uncommon; breeds from 9,000 to 10,000 feet; more common in winter than summer.

334a. =Western goshawk.= ACCIPITER ATRICAPILLUS STRIATULUS. Winter visitor; rare, if not accidental; Pacific Coast form; comes regularly as far east as Idaho.

337a. =Krider's hawk.= BUTEO BOREALIS KRIDERII. Resident; not uncommon; nests on the plains; no certain record for the mountains.

337b. =Western red-tail.= BUTEO BOREALIS CALURUS. Abundant resident; this is the Rocky Mountain form, of which Krider's hawk is the eastern analogue; the ranges of the two forms overlap on the Colorado plains; calurus breeds from plains to 12,000 feet; not a few winter in the State.

337d. =Harlan's hawk.= BUTEO BOREALIS HARLANI. Rare

winter visitor; one specimen; natural habitat, Gulf States and lower Mississippi Valley.

339b. =Red-bellied hawk.= BUTEO LINEATUS ELEGANS. Rare migrant; Pacific coast species.

342. =Swainson's hawk.= BUTEO SWAINSONI. Common resident; breeds everywhere below 11,000 feet.

347a. =American rough-legged hawk.= ARCHIBUTEO LAGOPUS SANCTI-JOHANNIS. Somewhat common winter resident; arrives from the north in November and remains till March.

348. =Ferruginous rough-leg.= ARCHIBUTEO FERRUGINEUS. Rather common resident; breeds on plains and in mountains; winters mostly on plains and along lower streams.

349. =Golden eagle.= AQUILA CHRYSAETOS. Resident; common in favorable localities; breeds from foothills to 12,500 feet; in winter on plains and also in mountains, often at 11,000 feet.

352. =Bald eagle.= HALLIAEETUS LEUCOCEPHALUS. Fairly common resident; mostly in mountains in summer; on plains in winter.

355. =Prairie falcon.= FALCO MEXICANUS. Not uncommon resident; breeds from plains to 10,000 feet; quite numerous in more open portions of western Colorado.

356. =Duck hawk.= FALCO PEREGRINUS ANATUM. Resident; not uncommon locally; breeds up to 10,000 feet.

357. =Pigeon hawk.= FALCO COLUMBARIUS. Summer

resident; not common; usual breeding grounds 8,000 to 9,000 feet; some breed on the plains.

358. =Richardson's merlin.= FALCO RICHARDSONII. Rare summer resident; not uncommon in migration; naturalists not quite sure that it breeds in the State; has been taken in summer at an altitude of 11,000 feet.

360. =American sparrow hawk.= FALCO SPARVERIUS. Abundant resident; the most common hawk from the plains to 11,000 feet; some winter in State; breeds throughout its range.

360a. =Desert sparrow hawk.= FALCO SPARVERIUS DESERTICOLUS. Resident, though rare; taken in Middle and South Parks.

364. =American osprey.= PANDION HALIAETUS CAROLINENSIS. Summer resident; not uncommon locally; breeds as high as 9,000 feet; has been taken in fall at an altitude of 10,500 feet.

365. =American barn owl.= STRIX PRATINCOLA. Resident; quite rare; a southern species rarely coming so far north as Colorado.

366. =American long-eared owl.= ASIO WILSONIANUS. Common resident; winters from plains to 10,000 feet; breeds from plains to 11,000 feet; eggs laid early in April.

367. =Short-eared owl.= ASIO ACCIPITRINUS. Resident, but not common; highest record 9,500 feet.

368. =Barred owl.= SYRNIUM NEBULOSUM. Resident; few records; one breeding pair found in the northeastern part of the

State.

369. =Spotted owl.= SYRNIUM OCCIDENTALE. Resident; not common; a little doubt as to its identity; but Mr. Aiken vouches for its presence in the State.

371. =Richardson's owl.= NYCTALA TENGMALMI RICHARDSONI. Rare winter visitor; a northern species.

372. =Saw-whet owl.= NYCTALA ACADICA. Resident; not uncommon; occurs throughout the State below 8,000 feet.

373. =Screech owl.= MAGASCOPS ASIO. Rare resident; the eastern analogue of the next.

373e. =Rocky Mountain screech owl.= MAGASCOPS ASIO MAXWELLI? Common resident; found from plains and foothills to about 6,000 feet; rare visitant at nearly 9,000 feet.

373g. =Aiken's screech owl.= MEGASCOPS ASIO AIKENI. Resident; limited to from 5,000 to 9,000 feet.

374. =Flammulated screech owl.= MEGASCOPS FLAMMEOLA. Rare resident; rarest owl in Colorado, if not in the United States; ten instances of breeding, all in Colorado; twenty-three records in all for the State.

375a. =Western horned owl.= BUBO VIRGINIANUS PALLESCENS. Common resident; breeds on the plains and in the mountains.

375b. =Arctic horned owl.= BUBO VIRGINIANUS ARCTICUS. Winter visitor; not uncommon; breeds in arctic America.

376. =Snowy owl.= NYCTEA NYCTEA. Rare winter visitor; occurs on the plains and in the lower foothills; range in summer, extreme northern portions of northern hemisphere.

378. =Burrowing owl.= **ATHENE CUNICULARIA** Resident; abundant locally; breeds on plains and up to 9,000 feet.

379. =Pygmy owl.= GLAUCIDIUM GNOMA. Resident; rare; favorite home in the mountains; breeds as high as 10,000 feet.

382. =Carolina paroquet.= CONURUS CAROLINENSIS. Formerly resident; few records; general range, east and south; now almost exterminated.

385. =Road-runner.= GEOCOCCYX CALIFORNIANUS. Resident; not common; restricted to southern portion of the State; breeds throughout its range; rare above 5,000 feet, though one was found in the Wet Mountains at an altitude of 8,000 feet.

387. =Yellow-billed cuckoo.= COCCYZUS AMERICANUS. Rare summer visitor, on the authority of Major Bendire.

387a. =California cuckoo.= COCCYZUS AMERICANUS OCCIDENTALIS. Summer resident; not uncommon locally; mostly found on the edge of the plains, but occasionally up to 8,000 feet in mountains.

388. =Black-billed cuckoo.= COCCYZUS ERYTHROPHTHALMUS. Rare migrant; only two records.

390. =Belted kingfisher.= CERYLE ALCYON. Common resident; breeds from plains to 10,000 feet; a few remain in winter.

393e. =Rocky Mountain hairy woodpecker.= DRYOBATES

VILLOSUS MONTICOLA. Common resident; breeds from plains to 11,000 feet; winter range almost the same.

394c. =Downy woodpecker.= DRYOBATES PUBESCENS MEDIANUS. Visitor; rare, if not accidental.

394b. =Batchelder's woodpecker.= DRYOBATES PUBESCENS HOMORUS. Common resident; breeding range from plains to 11,500 feet; winter range from plains to 10,000 feet.

396. =Texan woodpecker.= DRYOBATES SCALARIS BAIRDI. Resident; rare and local; southern range generally.

401b. =Alpine three-toed woodpecker.= PICOIDES AMERICANUS DORSALIS. Resident; not common; a mountain bird; range, 8,000 to 12,000 feet; even in winter remains in the pine belt at about 10,000 feet.

402. =Yellow-bellied sapsucker.= SPHYRAPICUS VARIUS. Rare migrant; eastern form, scarcely reaching the base of the Rockies.

402a. =Red-naped sapsucker.= SPHYRAPICUS VARIUS NUCHALIS. Common summer resident; breeds from plains to 12,000 feet, but partial to the mountains. Author saw one at Green Lake.

404. =Williamson's sapsucker.= SPHYRAPICUS THYROIDEUS. Common summer resident; breeds from 5,000 feet to upper limits of the pines; range higher in the southern part of the State than in the northern.

405a. =Northern pileated woodpecker.= CEOPHLOEUS PILEATUS ABIETICOLA. Resident; very rare; only probably identified.

406. =Red-headed woodpecker.= MELANERPES ERYTHROCEPHALUS. Common summer resident; breeds from plains to 10,000 feet; late spring arrival; same form in the East and West.

408. =Lewis's woodpecker.= MELANERPES TORQUATUS. Common resident; characteristic bird of the foothills; sometimes seen as high as 10,000 feet in southern Colorado; probably does not breed above 9,000 feet.

409. =Red-bellied woodpecker.= MELANERPES CAROLINUS. Summer visitor; rare, if not accidental; eastern and southern species, not occurring regularly west of central Kansas.

412a. =Northern flicker.= COLAPTES AURATUS LUTEUS. Rare migrant; range extends only to foothills; no record of its breeding.

413. =Red-shafted flicker.= COLAPTES CAFER. Abundant summer resident; breeds from plains to 12,000 feet; almost as plentiful at its highest range as on the plains; early spring arrival; a few winter in the State.

418. =Poor-will.= PHALÆNOPTILUS NUTTALLII. Common summer resident; breeds from plains to 8,000 feet; has been noted up to 10,000 feet.

418a. =Frosted poor-will.= PHALÆNOPTILUS NUTTALLII NITIDUS. Rare summer resident; few typical nitidus taken; a more southern variety.

420a. =Western nighthawk.= CHORDEILES VIRGINIANUS HENRYI. Abundant summer resident; breeds on the plains and up to about 11,000 feet; in fall ranges up to 12,000 feet; most common on plains and in foothills.

422. =Black swift.= CYPSELOIDES NIGER BOREALIS. Summer resident; abundant locally; southwestern part of the State; breeds from 10,000 to 12,000 feet, and ranges up to 13,000 feet.

425. =White-throated swift.= AERONAUTES MELANOLEUCUS. Summer resident; not uncommon locally; breeds in inaccessible rocks from 6,000 to 12,000 feet, if not higher; most common in southern part of the State.

429. =Black-chinned humming-bird.= TROCHILUS ALEXANDRI. Summer resident; local; only in southwestern part of the State, and below 6,000 feet.

432. =Broad-tailed humming-bird.= SELASPHORUS PLATYCERCUS. Common summer resident; Colorado's most common hummer; breeds from foothills to 11,000 feet; ranges 2,000 feet above timber-line in summer.

433. =Rufous humming-bird.= SELASPHORUS RUFUS. Summer resident; local; a western species, coming into southwestern Colorado, where it breeds from 7,000 to 10,000 feet, and ranges in summer several thousand feet higher; a few records east of the range.

436. =Calliope humming-bird.= STELLULA CALLIOPE. Summer visitor; rare or accidental; but two records, one near Breckenridge at an altitude of 9,500 feet; western species.

443. =Scissor-tailed flycatcher.= MILVULUS FORFICATUS. Summer visitor; rare or accidental; but one record; southern range, and more eastern.

444. =Kingbird.= TYRANNUS TYRANNUS. Common summer resident; occurs only on plains and in foothills up to 6,000 feet; same form as the eastern kingbird.

447. =Arkansas kingbird.= TYRANNUS VERTICALIS. Common summer resident; more common in eastern than western part of the State; fond of the plains and foothills, yet breeds as high as 8,000 feet.

448. =Cassin's kingbird.= TYRANNUS VOCIFERANS. Common summer resident; breeds on plains and up to 9,000 feet in mountains; occurs throughout the State.

454. =Ash-throated flycatcher.= MYIARCHUS CINERASCENS. Rare summer resident; western species, coming east to western edge of plains.

455a. =Olivaceous flycatcher.= MYIARCHUS LAWRENCEI OLIVASCENS. Summer visitor, rare, if not accidental; a southern species; taken once in Colorado.

456. =Phoebe.= SAYORNIS PHOEBE. Rare summer visitor; comes west to eastern border of the State.

457. =Say's phoebe.= SAYORNIS SAYA. Common summer resident; most common on the plains; occurs on both sides of the range; the author found it a little above Malta, at Glenwood, and in South Park.

459. =Olive-sided flycatcher.= CONTOPUS BOREALIS.

Common summer resident; breeds only in the mountains, from 7,000 to 12,000 feet.

462. =Western wood pewee.= CONTOPUS RICHARDSONII. Common summer resident; most common in breeding season from 7,000 to 11,000 feet.

464. =Western flycatcher.= EMPIDONAX DIFFICILIS. Common summer resident; breeds from plains to 10,000 feet, but most common in upper part of its range.

466. =Traill's flycatcher.= EMPIDONAX TRAILLII. Fairly common summer resident; most common on the plains, but occurs in mountains up to 8,000 feet; breeds throughout its Colorado range.

467. =Least flycatcher.= EMPIDONAX MINIMUS. Rare migrant; west to eastern foothills; probably breeds, but no nests have been found.

468. =Hammond's flycatcher.= EMPIDONAX HAMMONDI. Common summer resident; comes east only to the western edge of the plains; breeds as high as 9,000 feet.

469. =Wright's flycatcher.= EMPIDONAX WRIGHTII. Abundant summer resident; breeds from 7,500 feet to 10,000.

474a. =Pallid horned lark.= OTOCORIS ALPESTRIS LEUCOLA. Abundant winter resident; literature on this bird somewhat confused on account, no doubt, of its close resemblance to the next; winters on the plains abundantly, and sparsely in the mountains.

474c. =Desert horned lark.= OTOCORIS ALPESTRIS

ARENICOLA. Abundant resident; winters on plains and in mountains up to 9,000 feet; breeds from plains to 13,000 feet; raises two broods.

475. =American magpie.= PICA PICA HUDSONICA. Common resident; breeds commonly on the plains and in the foothills and lower mountains; a few breed as high as 11,000 feet.

478b. =Long-crested jay.= CYANOCITTA STELLERI DIADEMATA. Common resident; seldom strays far east of the foothills; breeds from base of foothills to timber-line; winter range from edge of plains almost to 10,000 feet.

480. =Woodhouse's jay.= APHELOCOMA WOODHOUSEI. Common resident; most common along the base of foothills and lower wooded mountains; sometimes breeds as high as 8,000 feet; in fall roams up to 9,500 in special instances.

484a. =Rocky Mountain jay.= PERISOREUS CANADENSIS CAPITALIS. Common resident; remains near timber-line throughout the year.

486. =American raven.= CORVUS CORAX SINUATUS. Resident; common locally; breeds; rather of western Colorado, but visitant among eastern mountains.

487. =White-necked raven.= CORVUS CRYPTOLEUCUS. Rare resident now; formerly abundant along eastern base of the front range and a hundred miles out on the plains; now driven out by advent of white man.

488. =American crow.= CORVUS AMERICANUS. Resident; common in northeastern Colorado; rare in the rest of the State.

491. =Clark's nutcracker.= NUCIFRAGA COLUMBIANA. Abundant resident; a mountain bird; breeds from 7,000 to 12,000 feet; sometimes in fall gathers in "enormous flocks"; at that season wanders up to at least 13,000 feet; most remain in the mountains through the winter, though a few descend to the plains.

492. =Pinon jay.= CYANOCEPHALUS CYANOCEPHALUS. Resident; abundant locally; breeds almost exclusively among the pinon pines; keeps in small parties during breeding season; then gathers in large flocks; wandering up to 10,000 feet.

494. =Bobolink.= DOLICHONYX ORYZIVORUS. Rare summer visitor.

495. =Cowbird.= MOLOTHRUS ATER. Common summer resident; breeds from plains to about 8,000 feet; author saw several in South Park.

497. =Yellow-headed blackbird.= XANTHOCEPHALUS XANTHOCEPHALUS. Common summer resident; breeds in suitable places on the plains and in mountain parks.

498. =Red-winged blackbird.= AGELAIUS PHOENICEUS. Common summer resident; breeds mostly below 7,500 feet, though occasionally ascends to 9,000.

501b. =Western meadow-lark.= STURNELLA MAGNA NEGLECTA. Abundant summer resident.

506. =Orchard oriole.= ICTERUS SPURIUS. Summer visitor; rare, if not accidental.

507. =Baltimore oriole.= ICTERUS GALBULA. Marked as a rare summer resident, though no record of nesting.

508. =Bullock's oriole.= ICTERUS BULLOCKI. Abundant summer resident; breeds on plains and in mountain regions below 10,000 feet.

509. =Rusty blackbird.= SCOLECOPHAGUS CAROLINUS. Migrant; rare, if not accidental; two records.

510. =Brewer's blackbird.= SCOLECOPHAGUS CYANOCEPHALUS. Abundant summer resident.

511b. =Bronzed grackle.= QUISCALUS QUISCULA 芏 EUS. Summer resident; not uncommon locally; comes only to eastern base of mountains.

514a. =Western evening grosbeak.= COCCOTHRAUSTES VESPERTINUS MONTANUS. Resident; found every month of the year; no nests found, but evidently breeds.

515a. =Rocky Mountain pine grosbeak.= PINICOLA ENUCLEATOR MONTANA. Resident; not uncommon; most common in late summer and fall when most of them are just below timber-line; stragglers descend to foothills and plains.

517. =Purple finch.= CARPODACUS PURPUREUS. Migrant; rare, if not accidental; only one specimen, and that a female.

518. =Cassin's purple finch.= CARPODACUS CASSINI. Common resident; winters from plains to 7,000 feet; breeds from that altitude to 10,000 feet.

519. =House finch.= CARPODACUS MEXICANUS FRONTALIS. Abundant resident.

521a. =Mexican crossbill.= LOXIA CURVIROSTRA STRICKLANDI. Resident; not uncommon; has been seen in summer at 11,000 feet; breeds in mountains, perhaps in winter like its eastern antitype.

522. =White-winged crossbill.= LOXIA LEUCOPTERA. Rare winter visitor; one record.

524. =Gray-crowned leucosticte.= LEUCOSTICTE TEPHROCOTIS. Rare winter visitor; western species.

524a. =Hepburn's leucosticte.= LEUCOSTICTE TEPHROCOTIS LITTORALIS. Rare winter visitor; summers in the North.

525. =Black leucosticte.= LEUCOSTICTE ATRATA. Rare winter visitor; summer range unknown; winters in the Rockies.

526. =Brown-capped leucosticte.= LEUCOSTICTE AUSTRALIS. This little bird and the white-tailed ptarmigan have the highest summer range of any Colorado birds.

528. =Redpoll.= ACANTHIS LINARIA. Common winter resident; lives from plains to 10,000 feet.

528b. =Greater redpoll.= ACANTHIS LINARIA ROSTRATA. Rare or accidental winter visitor; one record.

529. =American goldfinch.= ASTRAGALINUS TRISTIS. Resident; quite common in summer; sometimes reaches 10,000 feet.

529a. =Western goldfinch.= ASTRAGALINUS TRISTIS PALLIDUS. Migrant; probably common; added by Mr. Aiken.

530. =Arkansas goldfinch.= ASTRAGALINUS PSALTRIA. Common summer resident; breeds from plains to over 9,000 feet.

530a. =Arizona goldfinch.= ASTRAGALINUS PSALTRIA ARIZON? Summer resident; not common.

530b. =Mexican goldfinch.= ASTRAGALINUS PSALTRIA MEXICANUS. Rare, but believed to be a summer resident at Trinidad.

533. =Pine siskin.= SPINUS PINUS. Common resident; breeding range from plains to timber-line.

000. =English sparrow.= PASSER DOMESTICUS. Rapidly increasing in numbers; has settled at points west of the range.

534. =Snowflake.= PASSERINA NIVALIS. Rare winter visitor; one record west of the range; several east.

536a. =Alaskan longspur.= CALCARIUS LAPPONICUS ALASCENSIS. Common winter resident; breeds far north.

538. =Chestnut-collared longspur.= CALCARIUS ORNATUS. Rare summer resident; winter resident, not common; common in migration.

539. =McCown's longspur.= RHYNCOPHANES MCCOWNII. Common winter resident, dwelling on the plains.

540a. =Western vesper sparrow.= POOECETES GRAMINEUS CONFINIS. Abundant summer resident; breeds from plains to 12,000 feet.

542b. =Western savanna sparrow.= AMMODRAMUS SANDWICHENSIS ALAUDINUS. Common summer resident; breeds from base of foothills to almost 12,000 feet.

545. =Baird's sparrow.= AMMODRAMUS BAIRDII. Migrant; not common; a number taken east of the range, and one west.

546a. =Western grasshopper sparrow.= AMMODRAMUS SAVANNARUM PERPALLIDUS. Not uncommon summer resident; breeds on plains and in lower foothills.

552a. =Western lark sparrow.= CHONDESTES GRAMMACUS STRIGATUS. Common summer resident; breeds on plains and in mountain parks to 10,000 feet.

553. =Harris's sparrow.= ZONOTRICHIA QUERULA. Rare migrant; abundant migrant in Kansas.

554. =White-crowned sparrow.= ZONOTRICHIA LEUCOPHRYS. Abundant summer resident.

554a. =Intermediate sparrow.= ZONOTRICHIA LEUCOPHRYS GAMBELII. Common migrant, both east and west of the range; breeds north of the United States.

557. =Golden-crowned sparrow.= ZONOTRICHIA CORONATA. Accidental winter visitor; Pacific Coast species; breeds in Alaska.

558. =White-throated sparrow.= ZONOTRICHIA ALBICOLLIS. Rare migrant; but three records.

559a. =Western tree sparrow.= SPIZELLA MONTICOLA OCHRACEA. Common winter resident; mostly on plains and in lower mountains.

560. =Chipping sparrow.= SPIZELLA SOCIALIS. Rare summer resident; common in migration; goes as far west as base of the mountains.

560a. =Western chipping sparrow.= SPIZELLA SOCIALIS ARIZON? Abundant summer resident; breeds from base of foothills to 10,000 feet.

561. =Clay-colored sparrow.= SPIZELLA PALLIDA. Summer resident; not uncommon; scattered over State east of mountains.

562. =Brewer's sparrow.= SPIZELLA BREWERI. Summer resident; not uncommon; breeds from plains to 8,000 feet.

566. =White-winged junco.= JUNCO AIKENI. Common winter resident; on plains and 8,000 feet up in the mountains.

567. =Slate-colored junco.= JUNCO HYEMALIS. Winter resident; not common; not found above 8,000 feet.

567b. =Shufeldt's junco.= JUNCO HYEMALIS CONNECTENS. Abundant winter resident; most common in southern part of the State; not uncommon elsewhere.

567.1. =Montana junco.= JUNCO MONTANUS. Winter visitor; not uncommon.

568. =Pink-sided junco.= JUNCO MEARNSI. Common winter resident; plentiful at base of foothills in winter; in spring ascend to 10,000 feet; then leaves the State for the North.

568.1. =Ridgway's junco.= JUNCO ANNECTENS. Rare winter visitor; one record.

569. =Gray-headed junco.= JUNCO CANICEPS. Abundant resident; breeds from 7,500 to 12,000 feet; sometimes rears three broods.

570a. =Red-backed junco.= JUNCO PHONOTUS DORSALIS. Rare migrant; abundant just south of State.

573a. =Desert sparrow.= AMPHISPIZA BILINEATA DESERTICOLA. Summer resident; not uncommon locally; found only in southwestern part of the State.

574a. =Sage sparrow.= AMPHISPIZA BELLI NEVADENSIS. Abundant summer resident; common on sage-brush plains of western and southwestern Colorado; ranges as far east as San Luis Park and north to Cheyenne, Wyoming.

581. =Song-sparrow.= MELOSPIZA FASCIATA. Rare migrant; found only at eastern border of State.

581b. =Mountain song-sparrow.= MELOSPIZA FASCIATA MONTANA. Common summer resident; a few remain on plains in mild winters; breeds from plains to 8,000 feet.

583. =Lincoln's sparrow.= MELOSPIZA LINCOLNI. Common summer resident; abundant in migration; breeds from base of foothills to timber-line.

584. =Swamp sparrow.= MELOSPIZA GEORGIANA. Accidental summer visitor; one record.

585c. =Slate-colored sparrow.= PASSERELLA ILIACA SCHISTACEA. Rare summer resident; only three records.

588. =Arctic towhee.= PIPILO MACULATUS ARCTICUS. Winter resident; not uncommon; comes to base of Rocky Mountains in winter; breeds in the North, as far as the Saskatchewan River.

588a. =Spurred towhee.= PIPILO MACULATUS MEGALONYX. Common summer resident; upper limit, 9,000 feet.

591. =Canyon towhee.= PIPILO FUSCUS MESOLEUCUS. Resident; common locally; all records from Arkansas Valley; rare at an altitude of 10,000 feet.

592. =Abert's towhee.= PIPILO ABERTI. Rare summer resident; species abundant in New Mexico and Arizona.

592.1. =Green-tailed towhee.= OREOSPIZA CHLORURA. Common summer resident; melodious songster.

593. =Cardinal.= CARDINALIS CARDINALIS. Winter visitor; rare, if not accidental; two records.

595. =Rose-breasted grosbeak.= ZAMELODIA LUDOVICIANA. Accidental summer resident; one record.

596. =Black-headed grosbeak.= ZAMELODIA MELANOCEPHALA. Common summer resident; breeds from plains to 8,500 feet; has been seen at 10,000 feet.

597a. =Western blue grosbeak.= GUIRACA CAERULEA LAZULA. Summer resident; not uncommon locally; southern part of State; author saw one pair at Colorado Springs.

598. =Indigo bunting.= CYANOSPIZA CYANEA. Rare summer visitor; range, farther east.

599. =Lazuli bunting.= CYANOSPIZA AMOENA. Abundant summer resident; does not breed far up in the mountains, but has been taken at 9,100 feet.

604. =Dickcissel.= SPIZA AMERICANA. Rare summer resident; only on plains and in foothills.

605. =Lark bunting.= CALAMOSPIZA MELANOCORYS. Abundant summer resident; very plentiful on the plains; sometimes breeds as far up in mountains as 9,000 feet.

607. =Louisiana tanager.= PIRANGA LUDOVICIANA. Common summer resident; in migration common on the plains, but breeds from 6,000 to 10,000 feet.

608. =Scarlet tanager.= PIRANGA ERYTHROMELAS. Rare migrant.

610a. =Cooper's tanager.= PIRANGA RUBRA COOPERI. Rare or accidental summer visitor; abundant in New Mexico and Arizona; only one record for Colorado.

611. =Purple martin.= PROGNE SUBIS. Summer resident; local; rare in eastern, quite common in western part of the State.

612. =Cliff-swallow.= PETROCHELIDON LUNIFRONS. Abundant summer resident; breeds everywhere from plains to 10,000 feet; nests on cliffs and beneath eaves.

613. =Barn swallow.= HIRUNDO ERYTHROGASTER. Common summer resident; breeds from plains to 10,000 feet.

614. =Tree swallow.= TACHYCINETA BICOLOR. Summer

resident; not uncommon; breeds occasionally on the plains; more frequently in mountains up to 10,000 feet.

615. =Violet-green swallow.= TACHYCINETA THALASSINA. Summer resident; abundant locally; a few breed on plains; more commonly from 6,000 to 10,500 feet.

616. =Bank swallow.= CLIVICOLA RIPARIA. Rare summer resident; rarest Colorado swallow; from plains to foothills.

617. =Rough-winged swallow.= STELGIDOPTERYX SERRIPENNIS. Summer resident; not uncommon; breeds below 7,500 feet.

618. =Bohemian waxwing.= AMPELIS GARRULUS. Winter resident; not uncommon; breeds north of the United States.

619. =Cedar waxwing.= AMPELIS CEDRORUM. Resident; not common; breeds from plains to about 9,000 feet.

621. =Northern shrike.= LANIUS BOREALIS. Common winter resident; on its return from the North in October it first appears above timber-line, then descends to the plains.

622a. =White-rumped shrike.= LANIUS LUDOVICIANUS EXCUBITORIDES. Common summer resident; breeds mostly on the plains; sometimes in mountains up to 9,500 feet.

624. =Red-eyed vireo.= VIREO OLIVACEUS. Rare summer resident; an eastern species, coming only to base of foothills; still, one was taken at 11,000 feet.

627. =Warbling vireo.= VIREO GILVUS. Common summer resident; breeds sparingly on the plains; commonly in mountains

up to 10,000.

629a. =Cassin's vireo.= VIREO SOLITARIUS CASSINII. Rare or accidental summer visitor; not known to breed; a southwestern species.

629b. =Plumbeous vireo.= VIREO SOLITARIUS PLUMBEUS. Summer resident; common; breeds in foothills and mountains up to over 9,000 feet.

636. =Black and white warbler.= MNIOTILTA VARIA. Rare summer visitor; two records.

644. =Virginia's warbler.= HELMINTHOPHILA VIRGINI? Common summer resident; western bird, but breeds along eastern base of foothills.

646. =Orange-crowned warbler.= HELMINTHOPHILA CELATA. Summer resident; not uncommon; common migrant; breeds from 6,000 to 9,000 feet.

646a. =Lutescent warbler.= HELMINTHOPHILA CELATA LUTESCENS. Summer resident; not uncommon: western form of the orange-crowned warbler; ranges to eastern base of mountains.

647. =Tennessee warbler.= HELMINTHOPHILA PEREGRINA. Rare migrant; eastern Colorado to base of mountains.

648. =Parula warbler.= COMPSOTHLYPIS AMERICANA. Rare summer resident; comes to base of foothills.

652. =Yellow warbler.= DENDROICA PETECHIA. Abundant summer resident; breeds up to 8,000 feet.

652a. =Sonora yellow warbler.= DENDROICA SONORANA. Summer resident; probably common; to the southwest.

654. =Black-throated blue warbler.= DENDROICA CAERULESCENS. Rare migrant; one record.

655. =Myrtle warbler.= DENDROICA CORONATA. Common migrant; scarcely known west of the range.

656. =Audubon's warbler.= DENDROICA AUDUBONI. Abundant summer resident; breeds from 7,000 to 11,000 feet.

657. =Magnolia warbler.= DENDROICA MACULOSA. Rare migrant; breeds northward.

658. =Cerulean warbler.= DENDROICA RARA. Rare migrant; one record.

661. =Black-poll warbler.= DENDROICA STRIATA. Rare summer resident; sometimes common in migration; one breeding record for the State--at Seven Lakes; altitude, 11,000 feet.

664. =Grace's warbler.= DENDROICA GRACI? Summer resident; common in extreme southwestern part of the State.

665. =Black-throated gray warbler.= DENDROICA NIGRESCENS. Summer resident; not infrequent; breeds in pinon hills near Carson City.

668. =Townsend's warbler.= DENDROICA TOWNSENDI. Summer resident; not uncommon; western species, coming east to base of foothills and a few miles out on plains; breeds from 5,500 to 8,000 feet in western Colorado; in fall it is found as high as 10,000 feet.

672. =Palm warbler.= DENDROICA PALMARUM. Rare or accidental migrant; one specimen seen.

674. =Oven-bird.= SEIURUS AUROCAPILLUS. Rare breeder, on Mr. Aiken's authority.

675a. =Grinnell's water thrush.= SEIURUS NOVEBORACENSIS NOTABILIS. Rare migrant; appearing from plains to 8,000 feet.

678. =Connecticut warbler.= GEOTHLYPIS AGILIS. Rare or accidental migrant; one record by Mr. Aiken.

680. =Macgillivray's warbler.= GEOTHLYPIS TOLMIEI. Common summer resident; breeds from base of foothills to 9,000 feet.

681. =Maryland yellow-throat.= GEOTHLYPIS TRICHAS. One taken at Colorado Springs by Mr. Aiken.

681a. =Western yellow-throat.= GEOTHLYPIS TRICHAS OCCIDENTALIS. Common summer resident, almost restricted to the plains; both sides of the range.

683. =Yellow-breasted chat.= ICTERIA VIRENS. Accidental summer visitor.

683a. =Long-tailed chat.= ICTERIA VIRENS LONGICAUDA. Common summer resident; scarcely found in the mountains, but frequent in the lower foothills and on the plains; never seen above 8,000 feet.

685. =Wilson's warbler.= WILSONIA PUSILLA. Abundant

summer resident; centre of abundance in breeding season, 11,000 feet; known to breed at 12,000 feet; also as low as 6,000.

685a. =Pileolated warbler.= WILSONIA PUSILLA PILEOLATA. Summer resident; not uncommon; Mr. Aiken thinks it as plentiful as preceding.

686. =Canadian warbler.= WILSONIA CANADENSIS. Rare or accidental migrant; one record by Mr. Aiken.

687. =American redstart.= SETOPHAGA RUTICILLA. Summer resident; not uncommon in eastern, rare in western, Colorado; breeds below 8,000 feet.

697. =American pipit.= ANTHUS PENSILVANICUS. Common summer resident; breeds only on summits of the mountains.

701. =American dipper.= CINCLUS MEXICANUS. Resident; common in favorite localities; one seen above timber-line in October.

702. =Sage thrasher.= OROSCOPTES MONTANUS. Summer resident; breeds from plains to nearly 10,000 feet; western species, coming east to mountain slopes.

703. =Mocking-bird.= MIMUS POLYGLOTTOS. Summer resident; common locally; mostly on plains, but sometimes reaches 8,000 feet.

704. =Catbird.= GALEOSCOPTES CAROLINENSIS. Common summer resident; from plains to 8,000 feet.

705. =Brown thrasher.= HARPORHYNCHUS RUFUS. Not uncommon as summer resident; almost restricted to the plains.

708. =Bendire's thrasher.= HARPORHYNCHUS BENDIREI. Summer resident; rare and local; south central part of State.

715. =Rock wren.= SALPINCTES OBSOLETUS. Common summer resident; breeds from plains to 12,000 feet.

717a. =Canyon wren.= CATHERPES MEXICANUS CONSPERSUS. Rare resident; one nest recorded.

719b. =Baird's wren.= THRYOMANES BEWICKII LEUCOGASTER. Rare summer resident.

721b. =Western house wren.= TROGLODYTES AEDON AZTECUS. Common summer resident; from plains to 10,000 feet; raises two broods, sometimes three.

722. =Winter wren.= ANORTHURA HIEMALIS. Rare resident; no nest found.

725a. =Marsh wren.= CISTOTHORUS PALUDICOLA. Summer resident; not uncommon; breeds from plains to 8,000 feet; some remain all winter in hot-water swamps.

725c. =Western marsh wren.= CISTOTHORUS PALUSTRIS PLESIUS. Summer resident; not uncommon locally.

726b. =Rocky Mountain creeper.= CERTHIA FAMILIARIS MONTANA. Common resident; in breeding season confined to the immediate vicinity of timber-line, where some remain the year round.

727. =White-breasted nuthatch.= SITTA CAROLINENSIS. Resident; not common.

727a. =Slender-billed nuthatch.= SITTA CAROLINENSIS ACULEATA. Common resident; western form; commonly breeds from 7,500 feet to timber-line.

728. =Red-breasted nuthatch.= SITTA CANADENSIS. Not uncommon resident; migrant on the plains; resident in the mountains to about 8,000 feet, sometimes 10,000.

730. =Pigmy nuthatch.= SITTA PYGMAEA. Abundant resident; mountain bird; makes scarcely any migration; most common from 7,000 to 10,000 feet.

733a. =Gray titmouse.= PARUS INORNATUS GRISEUS. Resident; not common; southern species, coming to eastern foothills.

735a. =Long-tailed chickadee.= PARUS ATRICAPILLUS SEPTENTRIONALIS. Not uncommon resident; winters on plains and in foothills; breeds from 7,000 to 10,000 feet; sometimes on plains.

738. =Mountain chickadee.= PARUS GAMBELI. Abundant resident; nests from 8,000 feet to timber-line; ranges in the fall to the tops of the loftiest peaks.

744. =Lead-colored bush-tit.= PSALTRIPARUS PLUMBEUS. Resident; not common; western species, coming to eastern foothills.

748. =Golden-crowned kinglet.= REGULUS SATRAPA. Rare summer resident; rather common in migration; breeds only near timber-line at about 11,000.

749. =Ruby-crowned kinglet.= REGULUS CALENDULA. Abundant summer resident; breeds from 9,000 feet to timber-line.

751. =Blue-gray gnatcatcher.= POLIOPTILA CERULEA. Rare summer resident; breeds on the plains and in the foothills.

754. =Townsend's solitaire.= MYADESTES TOWNSENDII. Common resident; breeds from 8,000 to 12,000 feet; winters in mountains, though stragglers are sometimes seen on the plains. The author saw a pair on plains near Arvada, in company with a young, well-fledged bird.

756a. =Willow thrush.= HYLOCICHLA FUSCESCENS SALICICOLA. Summer resident; rather common; breeds in foothills and parks up to about 8,000 feet.

758a. =Olive-backed thrush.= HYLOCICHLA USTULATA SWAINSONII. Rare migrant.

758c. =Alma's thrush.= HYLOCICHLA USTULATA ALAM? Rare summer resident; in migration common.

759. =Dwarf hermit thrush.= HYLOCICHLA AONALASCHK? Rare migrant.

759a. =Audubon's hermit thrush.= HYLOCICHLA AONALASCHK?AUDUBONI. Common summer resident; breeds from 8,000 feet to timber-line.

759b. =Hermit thrush.= HYLOCICHLA AONALASCHK?PALLASII. Rare migrant; comes to the eastern edge of Colorado, just touching range of auduboni.

761. =American robin.= MERULA MIGRATORIA. Summer

resident, but not common; some interesting questions arise in connection with intermediate forms.

761a. =Western robin.= MERULA MIGRATORIA PROPINQUA. Abundant summer resident; breeds from plains to timber-line.

765a. =Greenland wheatear.= SAXICOLA OENANTHE LEUCORHOA. European species; a straggler taken at Boulder by Minot.

766. =Bluebird.= SIALIA SIALIS. Rare summer resident; west to base of Rockies.

767a. =Chestnut-backed bluebird.= SIALIA MEXICANA BAIRDI. Summer resident; not common; western form, coming east as far as Pueblo.

768. =Mountain bluebird.= SIALIA ARCTICA. Abundant summer resident; breeds from plains to timber-line; in autumn roams up to at least 13,000 feet.

THE END

www.ingramcontent.com/pod-product-compliance
Lightning Source LLC
Chambersburg PA
CBHW070108290526
45789CB00005B/1963